PENGUIN BOOKS

THE CHILDREN AT SANTA CLARA

Elizabeth Marek, born in 1961 in New York City, was graduated from Harvard College in 1984. She worked at a school for emotionally disturbed children in New York City. She is currently a student of the School of Clinical Psychology at New York University.

The Children at Santa Clara

ELIZABETH MAREK

PENGUIN BOOKS

PENGUIN BOOKS
Published by the Penguin Group
Viking Penguin Inc., 40 West 23rd Street,
New York, New York 10010, U.S.A.
Penguin Books Ltd, 27 Wrights Lane,
London W8 5TZ, England
Penguin Books Australia Ltd, Ringwood,
Victoria, Australia
Penguin Books Canada Ltd, 2801 John Street,
Markham, Ontario, Canada L3R 1B4
Penguin Books (N.Z.) Ltd, 182–190 Wairau Road,
Auckland 10, New Zealand

Penguin Books Ltd, Registered Offices:
Harmondsworth, Middlesex, England

First published in the United States of America by
Viking Penguin Inc., 1987
Published in Penguin Books 1988

LIBRARY OF CONGRESS CATALOGING IN PUBLICATION DATA
Marek, Elizabeth.
The children at Santa Clara.
1. Mentally ill children—Care—United States—
Case studies. 2. Child psychotherapy—Residential
treatment—Case studies. I. Title.
[RJ504.5.M37 1988] 362.2'088055 87-32842
ISBN 0 14 01.1118 2

Printed in the United States of America by
R. R. Donnelley & Sons Company,
Harrisonburg, Virginia
Set in Trump Mediaeval
Designed by Beth Tondreau

To my parents
who held me close and then let me go
and
to the children
who taught me how to hold

Acknowledgments

I am deeply grateful to Mira Rothenberg, whose love and enthusiasm for these special children pointed me in their direction, and whose kindness made my experiences possible. I am also indebted to the staff of Santa Clara, without whose guidance and support I would have been on the next plane home. To my editor, Elisabeth Sifton, and to her assistant, Julie Dolin, who provided not only brilliant editing but also support for a first-book ego, I offer my profound appreciation and respect. And to Marc, for the hours spent listening and learning to care about this alien part of me, for the support and advice, for all the phone calls, my thanks are not enough, and I offer instead my love.

Author's Note

This is a work of nonfiction. The children described are real people, with whom I lived and worked and learned—people whom I learned to love. To protect their privacy and the privacy of the adults in the book, all names of people and places, except my own, have been changed. In addition, a number of incidents and all identifying characteristics have been fictionalized.

The Children at Santa Clara

Arrival

The room is too small for the activity it holds. The rain and the sucking spring mud outside have precluded the horseback riding we promised and the kids, blaming us, are sullen and uncooperative. Clay flies through the air as Alex sneaks up behind Peter and brings his fist down hard into the middle of the tower that Peter is building; Peter cries; Joe rests his boots on the table and slowly rubs his crotch, leering at Cindy; Mike shreds bits of paper from his notebook and wads them up with his spit, then throws them into Tracy's hair where they alight like tiny insects, his laughter harsh in the damp, dim room; Philip sits hunched over the desk, chewing his lip as he manipulates the buttons on his watch; James watches it all from his desk at the end of a row, his eyes barely visible under their lowered lids; and Paul rocks quietly in his corner.

I have a headache. It is impossible to light the room properly on days like today: the light from the single bulb hanging from the ceiling is absorbed into the thick, adobe walls like liquid seeping into a towel. The L-shaped room, designed more for privacy than learning, offers Alex a perfect vantage point from which to torture the other kids without being caught. On one wall there is a picture of an Indian woman, carrying corn to be ground at the pueblo. A jagged line of Scotch tape runs across the middle of her stomach where the poster was torn by tow-headed Lee who declared one day that only gringos were allowed to be on the walls. The other wall is bare except for an old clock, whose minute hand waits the full fifty-nine seconds before sighing and heaving itself on to the next minute with a mighty click. Philip often begs for a clock with a second hand, and watches anxiously as the minute hand inches along its journey, terrified that one day, one minute, it will grow tired and stop dead in its tracks.

Whoever built this room would probably be surprised by its current incarnation: a schoolhouse for emotionally and behaviorally disordered adolescents, and their twenty-year-old East Coast teacher, a refugee from a suspended Harvard education. I am often surprised to find myself in the room. When I boarded the airplane in New York in the beginning of January it had been cold and snowy. My mother and I had struggled to scrape the ice off the windshield so she could drive me to the airport. Three hours later I arrived in Las Cordilleras, a small city in the Southwest. The airport was tiny, its one squat building constructed of adobe. Everyone wore a cowboy hat and boots, and most had large turquoise and silver buckles studding their waists. It was warm and sunny, and the mountains looked rough and close against the blue sky. I walked outside, carrying my backpack over my shoulder, and made my way to the bus stop. I looked at the denim-covered man standing next to me, and asked in my most polite traveling voice which bus would take me into the center of town. He answered, and I was surprised that he had spoken in English. It seemed the most foreign place I had ever been. I watched the sun on the mountains as I waited for my bus.

In town I ate some lunch, killing time until three o'clock, the hour at which I had agreed to call my prospective employer, Mr. Dan Johnson, director of the Santa Clara Child Care Center. I strolled down the main street, watching the cars cruise by with their bellies practically scraping the ground. As I squinted along the vista of neon, I thought how ugly it was, this town, and how strange to find such ugliness in the midst of the beauty of the mountains—like a rusty beer can thrown into a sparkling pool. I was frightened, fully aware that this man—one I had never met—felt that he was doing me a favor by accepting my services at his facility for a year, my willingness to work for room and board only notwithstanding. I felt that he was granting me a favor as well, allowing me to gain experience in the field, and, more importantly, providing an escape from the unhappiness and confusion that I had been feeling at college.

I found a pay phone, loaded it with change, and carefully dialed the number. I was unsure that he would remember me, and I felt my mouth grow dry. The phone began to ring, and I fought the urge to hang up.

"Hello?" It was a child's voice, shouted into the receiver. I pulled my ear away.

"Uh, hi. Is Dr. Johnson there?"

"Who?"

"Dan Johnson? The—"

There was a scream on the other end, and an adult voice saying "You must *not* answer the phone, Cheryl," and then, to me, "Hi. Sorry. Can I help you?"

"I hope so," I said, suddenly doubtful. "I'm trying to reach Dr. Johnson . . ."

Silence. Then, "Oh, Dan?"

Dan Johnson was the director of the center, and I wondered why these people sounded so surprised when I asked for him. It was not until much later that I found out he did not have a Ph.D. and was never referred to as "doctor," although he had introduced himself to me with that title.

"Uh, yes," I said.

"Sure, sure. Hang on a sec. And you are?"

I had prepared my speech. "My name is Elizabeth Marek," I said, conscious of my voice rising at the end of my own name, a question. "I was hired by Dr. Johnson to come work at the school."

"School?"

"Uh, yeah. I thought . . ." My voice faded. Hadn't Dr. Johnson told anyone that I was coming? I felt like an intruder and wanted to slip quietly back into the sunshine outside, to be at home with friends and family who did not, at least, make me feel as though I were speaking a different language.

There was a long pause on the other end of the phone, and then the voice said, "Well, look. I don't know. Maybe you'd better just talk to Dan. Hang on, I'll get him."

"Thanks," I said, but the phone was already far from the voice, lying on some table. From the high-pitched shrieks and laughter in the background, I pictured a roomful of children chasing each other in circles. I wondered what I had gotten myself into.

"Elizabeth?" I was startled by the man's voice in my ear. In my mind, the phone lay on the table still, like a helpless Indian surrounded by a tribe of warring braves.

"Yes. Hello. Dr. Johnson?"

"Yes."

The conversation was at a standstill. I shoveled in a few more quarters, and began, "Uh, here I am. I'm in Las Cordilleras."

"Oh right, right. Well, look. Things are kind of crazy up here right now, what with a couple of our staff out sick and all, and I don't think we're gonna be able to get down there to fetch you for a while . . ."

"That's all right," I said politely. "I can just take a bus or whatever is easiest for you."

"No, no," he said. "We'll come get you, all right. Why don't you just hang out for a day or two, and then give me a call. Maybe tomorrow. And we'll see what we can work out."

What did he mean, I thought. On his instructions I had traveled two thousand miles. I was in Las Cordilleras, for Christ's sake, knowing nobody, surrounded by mountains. The closest ocean was a thousand miles away; the closest friend farther still. Just what did he expect me to do?

"Well . . ." I said.

"You can take care of yourself for a few days, can't you?"

It was a challenge. Either I was a child, as much in need of supervision as the kids I had come to look after, or I was an adult, able to look after myself.

"Oh, sure," I said. "No problem. Really."

"Tell you what. I'm bringing a group of kids in to the circus on Sunday. Why don't you meet us then. Twelve o'clock, in front of the civic center. Okay?"

I thought, frantically. Today was what, Friday? It

wouldn't be fun, but I could do it. After all, I had no choice. I found myself annoyed: he had, after all, set the date of my arrival. But he was my boss. "Twelve o'clock. Civic center," I repeated. "That sounds fine."

"And then on the trip up, we'll figure out something for you to do up here." He laughed, and I cringed. "Okay?"

"Okay. See you Sunday."

"See you Sunday," and he was gone.

I hung up the phone and shouldered my knapsack again, feeling the ache across my back as I started up the street in search of a cheap hotel. Cars honked as I walked along, and offers of rides, rooms and more were shouted at me in coarse, thick voices. I began to sweat under the Irish wool sweater that had been comfortable in the freezing New York winter, and I chewed the inside of my mouth to keep from crying. Fiercely, I told myself that this was an adventure, that I was glad I had come.

On the right I saw a sign for the San Fernando Motel, ten dollars a night, and I thought, what the hell, how bad can it be, it's only for a little while. I walked into the reception area and a small, scruffy dog ran up to me. I reached down to pet him and he bit me on the wrist, breaking the skin. Four red dots of blood appeared, like a TB test, and pain surged up into my elbow. He bites, the proprietress said, having finished screaming at her small child to "git." I told her I had found that out, and asked if he had rabies or anything. She said she was pretty sure he did not, and we left it at that.

She showed me to my room then, a large space with a sagging double bed covered by a dirty blanket and topsheet, a bilingual, English/Spanish Bible lying on a dusty desk, and a picture of Christ bleeding on a cross. I am here, I thought. I am in the Southwest. I am far, far away from home. I thanked the woman and told her it looked fine, and then she left and I lay down on the bed and thought about why I was there.

In many ways, I do not know, will probably never know. There were events, bad things that had happened. I had broken up with my boyfriend of six years, when he had said for the fiftieth time that he wasn't sure if he loved me and I had replied to his shock that I was no longer sure whether I loved him, either, and thought it would be best if we stopped seeing each other. My best friend, Rachael, was deep in an unhappy love affair and sat in her room all day listening to Joan Armatrading records and knitting enormous scarves in blood red wool, refusing to let anyone help. My roommate, Eve, appalled by my moping, yelled at me to stop whining, pull myself up by my bootstraps and get involved in something. And I escaped into the kind, strong arms of a blue-eyed senior who got me drunk and made love to me in front of the fire and gave me warm hugs and was as unable as I to understand why I woke up crying, night after night.

There was also an academic slump, a feeling that I was stupid, even in the face of an honors record. I had wriggled my way into a senior seminar on early American literature and was in way over my head with people who had all studied the subject before and wanted to explore it in more depth. I had never heard of Jonathan Edwards; what's more, once I began to study him I found him dull. I felt the same about James Fenimore Cooper and only a little better about Nathaniel Hawthorne. I had scribbled in my brown notebook through the endless hours, trying desperately to keep up with the flow of the discussion. I spoke often, offering my opinion, but the teacher merely smirked, saving the full brightness of his smile for the brilliant blond girl on my left, whom he had taught before, and thought highly of, as he told us all on the first day to her pleased embarrassment. She had blushed, and I had hated her. I had determined then and there to be as bright as she, but it had not worked.

But when I was honest with myself, I knew that it was none of these things, not even the totality of them, that had convinced me it was time to go away for a year. More than anything it had been a sense that I had lost my self, submerged it in a sea of demands and expectations. I had made myself up according to too many scripts. I was the understanding girlfriend for my lover, the cheerful friend for Rachael and Eve, the sane, successful daughter for my parents. If I stopped playing any of those roles, there, at Harvard, at home, I risked losing the love I knew in my heart was based on their convincing enactment. But if I could get away, go somewhere that no one knew me, I would be free to invent myself for myself, to make myself over, at last, in my own image. The understanding woman and dutiful daughter and caring friend would remain, I felt sure, but there would also be a person with her own needs and wants, who might get angry at demands when they were too great, instead of caving in to them.

There was nothing so well formed in my mind at the time I left, only an overwhelming urge to get away. The vague need had coalesced one day in the seminar, when I had been, I thought, particularly stupid. I had walked out of class that November afternoon and stood outside Seaver Hall wondering what I should do next. It was two o'clock in the afternoon and I had a lot of work to do. I took a few steps toward Lamont Library, where I could do the reserve reading for the seminar. But I was sick of Benjamin Franklin and angry at the professor for not thinking me the smartest, so I turned, and started toward Robinson to get the reading I had to do for my political philosophy course. But I was unable to stand the thought of Plato right then, either, so I started walking forward toward my dorm, when the image of Rachael knitting in time to the endless sameness of the music made me turn again and finally just plop myself down in the sun and cry. I had taken out a different small brown notebook, then, and spewed self-loathing in green ink onto its pages, the letters blurred by the blobs of tears. Halfway down the page, the words broke off in midsentence, and I covered them with black lines until they were barely discernible.

I had decided then to leave school for a year, and told my parents my decision that night on the phone. "You're running away," my father said and I said yes, you're right, as far and as fast as I can, so long, I'll see you when I get back. My parents had not liked it, my purposeless flight, so my father found me a job through a friend. It was in the Southwest and it sounded fine to me. I got through the rest of the semester curled up in a corner of Rachael's bed, listening to the rhythms of the music as she taught me how to knit, or cutting classes with her and walking by the river, laughing at the freedom of not caring, or pretending not to care. We made it through together, but when, alone and frightened, I finally boarded the plane on that icy afternoon, I was not at all sure that I was doing the right thing.

I was awakened from my reverie by a large bug, probably a spider, maybe a roach, trying to crawl into my mouth. Sputtering, I got up, took a shower in a trickle of rusty water, and went about the business of killing time until I could go and meet my new boss at the circus. As I ate and went sightseeing, and bought cheap turquoise jewelry from the Indians in Olde Towne, and watched myself from afar as I went through these motions, I found myself thinking that I had been right to come after all, despite the less than auspicious beginning.

I got through the days, alternating between the wild surges of excitement and panic and the slow ebbs of loneliness, until finally Sunday morning arrived. I splurged, taking a taxi to the civic center for close to five dollars. At twelve-fifteen, two large vans pulled up and forty kids got out, shepherded by six adults. I guessed that the kids, black, white, Indian, Hispanic, ranged in age from about five to fifteen. I smiled shyly at one, and asked if they were the kids from Santa Clara.

"Uh-uh, man," one little boy said. "The Santa Clara kids are the crazy ones. We're from the farm."

"Oh," I said, thoroughly confused. "And is Dan—"

"I'm Dan Johnson, " said a man, stepping toward me as he gently pushed the kids away and shouted directions over his shoulder. "Are you Liz?"

I nodded, extending my hand which he shook with a measured firmness. His smile was a little too wide, and his eyes avoided mine, looking out past my ear.

"Good," he said. "Let's get the kids settled inside, and then we can talk."

As soon as we had gotten ourselves arranged inside, though, the circus began, and I found myself surrounded by crawling, clinging kids, who swarmed into my lap for hugs and fed me popcorn and asked me to shell their peanuts for them as if they had known me for years. "Are you going to come live with us?" they asked, over and over, and fought about which cabin I would be in, whose counselor I would be, where I would eat and sit and sleep as I kept repeating, again and again, "I don't know. Whatever Dan decides. I just don't know." The circus lights dimmed and millions of tiny red bulbs soared in circles as I watched them and retrieved flashlights that slipped under seats and stopped cotton candy fights before they started and wished that I knew at least some of the answers to the questions that the children would not stop asking.

It was not until the bus trip back up to the farm, not until we had climbed high into the mountains past Tres Cruces and had fewer than sixty miles to go before I got to the place where I would be living for the next year, that Dan called me away from the kids to the front of the van and began to tell me about his decisions. He told me, first of all, that he had no idea what I was going to be doing and that he had allowed me to come only as a favor to his friend, Ruth, who knew me through my father. He said he hoped I would not get in the way. He told me that the center was divided into two sections, a farm and a residential treatment center, called the RTC, located about thirty miles apart. Most of the hundred-or-so kids who lived at the farm, with him and his family, were emotionally okay and needed only a foster home because their parents had abandoned them or could not care for them for one reason or another. The RTC, which housed only seven or eight kids at any given time, was for short-term care, offering six- to eighteen-month confinements for children with more serious emotional problems. A few of the farm kids were so violent and disruptive that the public school refused to educate them. These five came down to the RTC for school five days a week, but otherwise the farm and the RTC were entirely separate.

Dan said that I would probably be more useful at the RTC, although the child-to-staff ratio there was already three to one, far lower than it was at the farm. I suspected that he simply wanted me as far away from him as possible, but I said it sounded fine. What did I know? I knew only that I was trying to escape, though I did not really know from what, and I figured the sicker the better. They dropped me off at the RTC, alone, on their way up to the farm.

A wad of paper hits me on the head, and I tell Mike to cut it out. He tells me in turn that today was supposed to be a fun day, and it isn't fucking fair of us to make them do any work. Life isn't fair, says Bernie my co-teacher. I ask Mike what would be fun, and he says he wants to paint a picture. It is a surprisingly reasonable request, and I say sure and bring out a huge roll of paper and spread it out across the floor, telling the kids that they are going to paint a mural, all together. There are groans, especially from Alex and Joe, but probably since their classmate and not I has suggested it, everyone complies. They sit in a rectangle, on all sides of the paper, the jars and dishes of paint spread out among them. Mike directs the action where he can, telling Peter and James and Tony what colors they should use, and what should be drawn where, and leaving Alex and Joe to do as they please. Peter hums, and Alex tells him to shut up. Joe gets paint on Cindy's shirt, and she slams down her brush, and goes to wash. James puts a dab of color on the end of his brush and touches it to the paper. He seems surprised to see a mark appear, and tries it again. Mike begins to tell a joke in the detached, distant voice of someone absorbed in something important occurring within himself, trying to maintain contact with the more superficial world of his friends. It is peaceful. I listen to the rain drumming down on the roof and suddenly feel warm and safe, and hope that the kids do, too.

I watch them as they work, their heads bent over the paper, their breath, visible in the cold damp of the room, rising like steam from a volcano. When had I begun to love them? Mike, his buck teeth thrust out in an obscene grin as he finishes another joke. Tracy, her rolls of fat flopping over her too-tight, blue corduroy pants, her tongue pointing through her teeth as she concentrates on the small figure she is drawing on the paper with green paint. Tall, thin James, smiling a small, fragile smile as he dips the brush he holds with tense, twisted fingers into one color after another and moves it carefully to create color on white paper where there had been none before. Philip, his watch tucked into a shirt pocket so it does not get dirty, painting a small black swastika in the upper-right-hand corner. Paul, not painting but watching it all from his corner as he rocks and gives not the slightest indication that he is watching. And Franklin, laughing loud, splashing brightly colored blobs into his space as Mike tells him to watch it, for Christ's sake. And the rest, each with his own sad stories to tell . . . yet all sitting here, survivors, together, painting bright colors onto a roll of white paper, spread out on the floor.

Mike announces that they are finished. They have done a good job and I tell them so, meaning it. The paper is covered with delicate shapes and splashes of color that harmonize surprisingly well. Tracy has drawn a house and flower and green girl in the mountains under a blue sky, and Mike's spaceship whizzes overhead, through Peter's white clouds and Franklin's brightly colored ones. James's small dabs look like multicolored birds, which hover over dense, slanting trees that Tony, his wrist curved in on itself, has painted next to Tracy's house. There are strange shapes, too: Alex has painted monsters and bugs and animals swallowing people in a Hieronymous Bosch–like composition in one corner, and Philip's swastika has grown more elaborate and somewhat disguised in the other. Through it all runs a white river, like milk flowing through the promised land. I am not sure who is responsible for it, but it adds a nice touch, drawing together the disparate forms.

Bernie is impressed with their drawing as well, and tells them it looks like the Japanese prints he has seen in a museum in Las Cordilleras. They smile, and Mike wonders aloud whether they can get this hung in a museum somewhere. Bernie tells them he doesn't know, but in the museum he was in, each print had a poem to go with it, a sort of explanation of the events and emotions in the picture. The kids, old campaigners, are not so easily fooled. They know what is coming next. Oh, no, Alex says, no way are you getting me to write a poem, and Joe nods yeah, because only fags do that. Franklin, a child whose very essence is filled with poetry, giggles at the word fag, and agrees that poems are only for *hoditos*. But Bernie talks of great Spanish poets, Indian poets, and finally tells them that he will not make each of them write his own poem but they will write one all together, just as they have painted. Mike likes this idea. Yeah, he says. We've drawn a Japanese poetry land. We need to write a poem . . . And so they do.

Mike begins. He stares at the spaceship he has drawn, and at Tracy's green girl underneath, and says, "There once was a martian." It is Alex's turn then, and he is still angry at

Mike, and says, "That didn't exist." Joe refuses to say anything, and goes off to hammer blocks of wood together in the corner. Bernie and I decide not to press him, and say "Come on, Peter, your turn next," but Peter does not know what to say, either, and we say, "Come on, just look at the picture, what do you see?" and finally he says, "People in there running." Franklin has been staring at the mural, *hoditos* forgotten, and dreamily he says, "With its radiant beauty." I wonder where he learned the word radiant and suddenly remember that Jason, the senior staff member, has been reading them *Charlotte's Web.* I smile at him and Tracy, seeing that, gives her line, saying "And all the pretty colors," and I smile at her, too. Tony has been staring at what Philip drew and finally smiles and says "An ex-swastika." Then it is Philip's turn. He has wanted to say something about what he had drawn, but Tony has done that already, so he looks at the shape that Tony has drawn in the sky, and says suddenly "God is coming to earth." James continues, his fingers twisted so tightly that they seem welded together, his voice a raspy whisper, "And the sun is mad." And then order and turns are forgotten, and the kids shout their lines one after another, faster and faster, all of them catching the rhythm they have created and carrying it forward. I watch them, and love them, and think how glad I am to be there, with them all, how long ago the day at the circus seems already.

When they have finished, Mike copies the poem out carefully in black ink onto a long piece of paper and, at the end, he writes proudly, by Philip, Peter, Tracy, Tony, Alex, James, Franklin, Mike. We hang up the picture and the poem, and the kids run down to the house and drag up Lois, the director of the RTC, and Jason, and they admire it sincerely. It stays there, on the wall, under the ancient clock, a symbol to all the kids of their achievement, for three days, until Joe rips it down and tears it to pieces.

These are my kids, these and a few others who had already come and gone before the Japanese poetry land. These are my kids, and the stories that follow are their stories.

Tracy

Whenever I twirl my fingers I still think of James. And think of Philip when I wind my watch, and when I feel the urge to hurt myself Corinne is there with me, and Franklin when I see the stars. I think of Tracy, though, hardly at all. Except to think, sometimes, how difficult she was in the mornings, when we would all be gathered around in the small kitchen, all sitting around the scratched and scarred wooden table, on the two long benches, when I would be mixing the batter for our muffins, and Bernie would be there at the stove, making jalapeño omelettes with the shells in for crunch, and giving a dollar to anyone who would eat them, which Franklin always would, and when Lois would be there, smoking and chattering and laughing, and hovering over the coffee pot, saying, "Where is Tracy?"

Tracy came in, soiled blue used Camp Tarrarack T-shirt clinging to her rolls of fat and burgeoning breasts, and dirty underwear and slippers. She stopped in the doorway, waiting, scratching her head through her ragged hair.

"Oh, my goodness, Tracy Sue," Lois said. "Nononono-nononono, dear. That is not how we dress for breakfast."

"Fuck you."

And Franklin jumped in, "Hey, Bernie! *Hodito!* She said it! She said it! Now she has to do her push-ups. Ten of 'em for a 'fuck,' right Bernie?" And punctilious Philip: "You know, Trace, you'd do a lot better if you would just remember to dress properly in the morning. You really should know by now . . . I mean, I arrived merely two weeks ago, and I already know the procedure. You've been here for a year already, and you don't even know it," as his words were drowned out by the noise of Bernie hauling Franklin over by the stove to do his push-ups for repeating Tracy's "fuck." Then Tracy lunged at Philip with claws bared and Jason—the rock and the redeemer as usual—stepped in to restore order, and I poured muffin mix into tins, and James sat with his fingers twirling, twirling.

But as I stood there, pouring my muffin batter and reminding myself how sick she was, such a very, very sick little girl, I still felt angry at her, at how every morning she burst the cocoon of stillness and peace that hangs around all early mornings, blending with the smell of coffee and sleep and gentle heat, and offering the rest of the children one of the few chances I felt they had to share the happiness of my life as it had been, as I knew I was so often forced to share the pain of theirs.

I had never liked Tracy much, though, and I knew in my unguarded moments that it went deeper than her morning scenes. I had found her the most difficult to like from the beginning, when Dan dropped me off at the low adobe house. She was the first one I met. Shivering in the sudden bite of the mountain wind, I had walked down the driveway toward the snow-covered, dust-red house, wondering whether they were expecting me, what I should say. A large sheepdog had run to me and barked, and I shoved him away. Dan had told me to find a woman named Lois, but instead I saw Tracy. She was sitting on a doghouse with her fat legs in too-tight pants hanging over the sides, as she clutched a cat.

"Hi," I said.

"Hi," she said, not looking up from the cat. "You're the new one, right? What's your name?" I started to tell her but she cut me off. "Mine's Tracy. I'm thirteen. This is my cat. He doesn't have a name yet. Not really. Just Cat, for now."

"Cat for now, huh?" I said. "That's a pretty silly name."

She glared at me then, a stare full of such rage that it hit me like a punch, and I took a step back. I felt shamed, and young, as though she knew more than I ever would or could and would never hesitate to use that knowledge against me.

But in the next second the glare was gone, and she smiled again coyly. "Actually," she said, "I'm the only one of the kids that's allowed to have a cat. It's because I don't really live here, you know?" She looked at the cat again, stroking his fur in long, regular movements. "I mean, I live here, but I'm not really one of them, if you know what I mean."

She paused, and I stood feeling awkward and scared, not knowing how to react, how to help, how to deal with the lie. I thought, Christ, I haven't been here five minutes and already I'm screwing up. And I badly wanted to succeed. So that even when she saved me, in a way, by continuing her story, the gratitude I felt only increased my confusion. But she went on, "Just because my parents died, see, a couple of years ago, and so I came here . . ."

I heard a man's voice calling "Tracy!" from inside the house. As she turned, she relaxed her hold on the kitten, who jumped off her lap and scuttered away into the bushes.

"Oh fuck!" said Tracy.

"What's the matter," I asked, and again I was punished for my ignorance by a withering glance.

"Nothing," she said. "Only I'm not supposed to let any of the other kids touch the cat, so I don't like him to get too far away. It's okay, though. I mean, he'll come back . . ." Her voice rose. It was a question.

"Sure."

"Tra-cy!" The voice was louder.

"Um," I said. "Don't you think you should go see what he wants?"

"What? Oh, you mean Jason? No, he's calling the other Tracy . . . Hey, do you want me to give you a tour of the house? See, you'll probably be spending the most time with me, since I'm the only girl. Well, except for Corinne, but as you'll see, she really doesn't count."

"Oh?" I asked, outsmarting. "What about the other Tracy?" Checkmate, kiddo, I thought somewhere inside myself. I've got you now. Just admit you're lying, stop all this craziness and . . . and stopped by the glare again, before she turned her eyes as from something too lowly to contemplate, and slid off her perch, shouting almost sweetly, "Holy cow, Jason, I'm coming, I'm coming. Keep your pants on, will you?" She turned to me once more and asked if I would come with her, and I followed. Totally, I realized, in her control.

From there, things got better. Or perhaps they only seemed to. Because she needed me to like her as much as I thought then that I needed her to like me. See, I could say then, she likes me. I'm doing all right. We've made friends. I'm succeeding. And through me she could say, See, she likes me. I have a friend. I am likable. Except that we did not like each other, not at all, but were held together only by need and self-doubt.

Still, it got us through the first few weeks.

Thoroughly seduced by her, I would let her win at endless backgammon games, joined by the red and black triangles that lay between us, pointing at us accusingly while James watched, laughing to himself, staring into his fingers. And she did give me a tour of the house.

"This is Corinne's room," she said, leading me into a small carpeted room with flowered curtains and a sturdy brown bunk bed. A girl lay curled on the bottom bunk, moaning to herself as she twirled her spit around in her fingers. The top bunk was made up with a sheet and blanket. "Who sleeps there?" I asked, and she said, "There, oh, this girl named Katie, but she's hardly ever here these days. I think they're gonna put her in the lock-up pretty soon," and then she stopped as the girl on the bottom bunk grew angry and jammed her fist into her mouth, biting into her own flesh with all her strength. Tracy was on her in a minute, pulling the girl's bloody hand away from her mouth. "She does that sometimes," she said, and led me out of the room.

Across the hall, she showed me "the boys' room," shared by Lee and Paul, neither of whom was in, which was good, she said, because if they had been they probably wouldn't have let us enter—they didn't like girls. The carpeting was the same in that room, but there were plaid spreads on each twin bed and matching curtains in the windows. A crooked model airplane lay on a dresser.

At the end of the hall was a larger room, "James's room," Tracy said. A tall, pale boy, James, I assumed, lay on his bed, flat on his back, staring at the ceiling and laughing softly. "He's a little out of it," Tracy said. "Kinda schizo." James did not appear to hear her.

Next came the bathrooms, the playroom, the kitchen, the living room, and finally a smaller room that opened off of it. "This is my room," she said. I remember the gagging in my throat as the stench of urine assaulted me from every corner. Seeing my disgust, she said, "Yeah, it smells in here a little, huh. But I don't mind. Because it's only the cat, see, he does it sometimes when I'm not here. And when you love something, you've got to be willing to put up with that kind of thing. Right?"

"Sure, Trace. That's nice," I said, but of course I knew for myself what Lois wasted no time in telling me later that day, that Tracy did it herself, alone at night, crouching in the corner and discoloring the rug with pools of her own warm pee.

I got the rest of the story on Tracy soon enough, and all the kids—the ten other staff members each talking about his or her "primary child," the one for which they served as case manager, therapist, and parent, initiating me into a world I was far from prepared to understand.

Jason began the discussion, his soft southern drawl gently shaping the routine of the day. There were five school staff members, he explained, who arrived each morning at seven to wake the kids, feed them breakfast, supervise chores, and then teach lessons at the schoolhouse up the road: math, English, history—

"Riot control," Bernie broke in, and the others laughed and nodded.

School was done at 2:45, and then the three afternoon staffers began—got the kids settled for rest, got them up again, cooked dinner, and kept them amused until bedtime. At eleven, the one staff person whose turn it was to do overnight kept watch until the routine began all over again the next morning.

As he talked, I found myself hoping I could be part of the play staff, the afternoon group. I had already heard how difficult the five farm kids who attended the RTC school could be, and I felt more comfortable with the crazier, but less openly aggressive, house kids.

Before I could say anything, Jason went on. "Since we're not paying you or anything, we should really let you choose what you want to do. But I'll tell you, where we need you most right now is up at the school, to help with the farm kids." I tried to smile bravely, and he breezed over my lack of enthusiasm. "You'll do fine. Don't worry. And since you'll be living with the house kids anyway, I'm sure you'll have plenty of time to get to know them."

"In all their glory," Bernie said.

I smiled again, and it was settled. And then they began to talk about the kids, peopling Jason's abstract world of time and schedules with strange shadows.

"Tracy," said Lois. "Let's start with her." She turned to me. "Be careful, Liz. I can already see her making demands on you and, believe me, she won't stop until you make her stop. Really. She'll burn you out, and quick, if you let her."

"Okay," I said, thinking, My god, how can you be so callous. The child obviously needs all the love and time she can possibly get. What else am I here for?

"She had an abusive father," Lois continued. "We don't know too much about the rest of it, except that when Tracy finally fought back, her parents decided she'd gone crazy, and they put her into St. Francis for a two-week diagnostic. And then disappeared. Word has it that they're in Canada somewhere—her mom was from Quebec, I think. But no one really knows."

I sat there in the kitchen, then, drinking my camomile tea and trying to imagine, to feel, to be a little girl alone and frightened in a hospital, counting off the days until the two weeks had passed, until my parents would come and save me. "And then disappeared . . ." I saw myself age eight at the summer camp to which I'd begged to go. I had been so homesick when I arrived that I immediately pleaded to go home again, only to be told by my well-meaning parents that it was only two weeks, and I should just stick it out and try to have a good time. I remembered how alone I'd felt, and how sure that I would never see either of them again, for they did not want me. I remembered, and thought I understood Tracy better than I had before, and that all our antipathies would disappear as a result. I resolved again to love her, to give her all the love I had, to make up for the loss she'd suffered, burnout or no.

And the others went on as we sat there in the warm, cluttered kitchen, through the beatings and the rapes and the closets and the suicides and the murders and the neglect. Until I couldn't feel anymore. Or react. Until I needed to giggle at images I couldn't comprehend. Until I began to build a wall.

"Enough?" asked Lois, seeing my tears.

"I guess."

"Don't worry," she said. "You'll get used to it. You have to. The trick is—don't feel sorry for them. That's really important. Just try to admire their strength and work through that. Not their weaknesses."

"Really," said Bernie, his gray eyes flashing. "Don't be afraid to give 'em shit. It's hard to believe, but they're really grateful for any limits you can set for them."

"Okay," I said, still thinking that love, enough love, must somehow be enough. And I could love them all, I thought, knowing what I know now. Even Tracy.

But I was wrong. In the next weeks, as I struggled to love her, to understand, to give, I felt sucked dry by her endless demands, her lies, her clinging, her blatant use of me to spite the others. "No," Tracy would say to Franklin, to James, to Katie, to Lee. "She's my friend. She's with me now. You can't play with her." I felt like the puppy I had had as a child: she was my dog, and no, brother dear, you cannot play with her, you'd only hurt her, you're too young, leave her alone. I told Tracy that I was there for them all, that I would be with her, but that the others needed me, too. And I'd be met with, "Bitch. Cunt. *Hodito. Puta.*" Or "Just one more game," or "How come you always favor the boys?" Or, most often, just with her glare.

Worse, the others soon picked up on her game. Wherever I went, there they all were, pecking, pecking at me, Prometheus, bound upon my rock.

"You're allowed to say no, you know," Jason said one afternoon, after a long day at school, as I was being dragged off to push them all on the swings.

"Oh, I know," I said, laughing. "But it's okay, really. I'm fine."

"Well, all right," he said. "Just make sure to take some time out for yourself, though."

"Oh yeah, yeah, I will. Don't worry." And we shot out the door.

And still, I thought that Tracy needed me. That she liked me. That we were making friends and, through that, that I was doing my job, and doing it well. After all, I sometimes thought, she wasn't the easiest person to be friends with.

One day, toward the end of April, as I was asking where in the godforsaken town I could get a decent haircut, Tracy offered her services.

"Um, no thanks," I said.

"But I cut Joan's hair. And I do a really good job, don't I, Joan?"

Joan was Tracy's primary, a round, motherly woman who seemed impervious to Tracy's lies and tantrums. I found her rather cold and always felt that she neither liked nor approved of me. But now she smiled and agreed with her charge. "Actually, she is very good hair cutter. And the price is right."

I looked at Joan's hair, long and straight down her back, just like mine. After all, I figured, straight hair isn't so hard to do.

"Well . . ."

"Oh, please, Lizard. Please. It's good practice for me, too. You see, I want to be a hairstylist when I grow up."

"Well, okay. But listen, Tracy, I just want a trim. All right? No more than an inch."

"Oh sure, sure. Just tell me how much you want off, that's all. That's what Joan always does. You have really beautiful hair, you know. I wouldn't cut that much off."

So Joan got the scissors, and we moved a chair outside, onto the porch. With pomp and circumstance, Tracy threw a towel around my neck and gently dampened my hair with a washcloth. Watching her, I could almost see her body swell with the pride of trust, and I was glad I'd agreed to do it.

"But listen," I said, as she took the scissors in her hand. "Remember. Just an inch. Do you know how big an inch is?"

In response, she held up her thumb and forefinger an inch apart.

"Right," I said. "Just like that." I relaxed, staring out at the mountains, still coated with snow, shimmering in the late spring sunshine. She combed the strands out straight one more time, and then snip, snip, snip.

"Liz!" said Lois, appearing in the doorway. "How much did you say you wanted cut off?"

"An inch or so," I said, swinging around.

"Well, you better tell her to stop then, because—" My hand reached up and clutched the ragged ends, an inch or so below my ear, bumping halfway across my neck into the long shiny untouched pieces.

It wasn't until that moment that I understood how much Tracy hated and resented me: for my age, so close to her's, for my long, straight hair, for my freedom, for my sanity. But at that moment, I did not even care why she had done it. It was enough that she had. I was furious.

Franklin peeked out from under Lois's arm and hooted. "*Hodito,* man. You should never have let that crazy near your hair! Oooo, you look funnee."

I sat, tears in my eyes. Behind me Tracy laughed and then quickly changed it to a semicough. I am going to do it, I thought. I am going to grab those scissors out of this crazy child's hands and hurt her, hit her, make her stop laughing. But angry as I was, it was more at myself than at her. She was the crazy one, the one who had no control over her actions. I was the one who, knowing it all, had still allowed myself to sit down in a chair before her, scissors in her hand. But I loved my hair, it was a part of me, my vanity, and she had hurt it. On purpose. And with the unerring accuracy to wound that all these children seemed to possess. I felt myself beginning to cry.

"Sorry, Liz—" she began, taking a few steps backward.

"Hoooo, man! Whatcha gonna do to her? Oooo, Tracy! You're gonna get it good, now, man."

"Liz—?"

"Franklin," I said. "You need to leave us alone now. Go on into the kitchen and help Joan with dinner."

"Oh, man . . ."

"Yes, dear. Come on." Lois grabbed him by the arm and led him into the house, leaving me alone with Tracy.

With their departure, a strange stillness settled over the porch. Battling back my own tears—of betrayal, of anger, of wounded vanity—it was hard to see her mounting panic. My eyes were focused on the mountains, and I was thinking of a time long ago, when I had fussed so much over having my hair combed that my mother had threatened to have it all cut off. Tracy, I suppose, was contemplating her doom. So we sat there, joined by the mountain breeze, in the sunshine, until finally she said, "I guess you hate me now, huh, Lizard?"

"No, I don't hate you," I said, thinking, of course not, but I am a little angry at you, and even more angry at myself.

"Well, so, what's my punishment?" she said.

Oh, god, I thought, remembering limits. But how could I punish her? I wanted her to understand why she had done it, as I felt I did, to see that she had been jealous, had wanted to hurt me, so that, by understanding, she might come to be able to control those feelings. But I had no idea how to get her to see that. And simply to punish the action, which had been largely my fault, after all, seemed strangely irrelevant. I looked at her. She shivered in the April chill and reached up to play with the fringes of her own ragged hair. I smiled at the gesture. "No punishment, Trace." I said. I saw her tense. "But I do think you need to figure out why you needed to do what you did. Maybe talk it over with me later, or with Joan or someone. Okay?"

"But I didn't need to do anything. My fingers just slipped."

Oh, give it up, kid, I thought. And again, wondered how I was supposed to confront the lie. I had been driven into the checkmate trap with her before and had emerged feeling beaten. Not again.

"Honest, " she said, in my pause. "Anyway, I think it looks better the way it is. Or at least it will, as soon as the little edges are smoothed out."

Little edges, I thought, feeling the uneven weight on my back. Who is she kidding? At a loss, I finally said, "Okay, look, I'm not mad at you. Really. No punishment. If your fingers slipped, they slipped. Accidents happen. But I do think you should talk about it later with Joan." Hey, way to pass the buck, kiddo, I thought. But then, I had been working with her for only three months, and I did not know what else to do.

"Really? No punishment?"

"Really."

"Well then . . . can I go help Joan?"

"Sure. Go ahead." And she went. Again, I felt inadequate, like a child, younger than they, and far too happy and loved to ever be able to break the barrier of reserve beyond which all our souls are guarded. It did not help when, later on, washing the dishes in the kitchen, I heard Tracy bragging to the boys that I had let her off scot-free, and heard their murmurs, spoken in sympathy, not envy. I remembered Bernie's admonition about limits but felt incapable of setting them. I began to tell myself that I was useless, and worse, for in my ignorance and awkwardness I was hurting as well as helping, and these were human lives I was using for my training ground.

We became symbols of each other's failures, I think, or at least I remember thinking that then. Or perhaps it was merely an acknowledgment that we knew each other too well, and it frightened both of us. Or perhaps it was the lie, the denial of anger and hurt, that I had, as so often before, allowed to mar a relationship because smoothing over was so much easier. Whatever the reason, after the haircutting incident Tracy and I grew distant. Far from seeking my attentions, she would shy away from me, burrowing instead into Jason's arms or Lois's or Joan's. And I busied myself with the boys, and thought of her, besides pity, with anger, as the one who destroyed the peace of the early mornings.

We remained separate throughout the throbbing warmth of the summer, always managing to be on opposite teams in softball, opposite sides of the swimming hole, opposite ends of the van. By September, we were strangers, polite and aloof. Even during the weekly group therapy sessions, when the children took turns acting out a meaningful or upsetting experience, I found her "plays" the most difficult to watch. As soon as I saw it was her turn I would tune myself out, barely listening as she directed the action. Instead, I concentrated on keeping the farm kids from acting up, Corinne from biting her fingers and her brother Paul from taking off his clothes. It was important, so Lois said, for everyone to attend these sessions, and there we all were—eight RTC kids, five farm kids, and the RTC staff—but someone had to orchestrate the peace.

All I saw on this particular Thursday was that Tracy, who was never very good at these minidramas, had set the scene with Bernie in the classroom. Philip and Franklin and James and a couple of the farm kids stood at one end, making faces to Mike on the couch, to show that they, at least, were too sane and too cool to get involved in anything this dumb if they didn't absolutely have to.

"Okay, Tracy," Lois said. "What next?"

"Well, Bernie's over there with the farm kids, and they're fighting, and I need to ask a question."

"Okay." Bernie and the kids began to act their parts, but Tracy remained silent. Watching a little more closely, I saw her eyes glaze over a little bit, and she retreated into herself in a way I had never seen her do. "I need to ask a question," she repeated.

"It's all right. You can ask it now."

"I need to ask a question."

"What question, babe?"

"But nobody's listening to me."

"Yes, we are. We're all listening. Go ahead."

There was a long pause, and Tracy took a step back.

"Tracy?"

"I can't."

"It's okay. It's okay, honey. Do you want someone else to be you? To ask it for you?"

And, out of nowhere, I heard her say, "Liz. Liz knows what I'm thinking," and she turned to me.

"Okay," Lois said. "Come on up here, Liz."

Frightened, not wanting to make a mistake, I did as I was told.

"Okay, Tracy. Tell her what you want her to ask Bernie for you."

"No. She knows." Oh, god, I thought. No. No, I don't. I don't know, I don't . . . but then, looking a her, I suddenly did know, know her soul, and mine, and the question I have needed to ask, that we all need to ask, and ask all the time with gestures and eyes and actions but never with words, because we are sane and civilized and you just don't ask these things, not in real life, and here she was pleading with me to ask, to verbalize.

"Do you love me?" I asked Bernie, and heard Tracy burst into sobs behind me. Mommy do you love me, daddy do you love me, friends and lovers innumerable and past, do you love me?

"Do you?" All through my life . . . and do you love me most and best and will you love me forever and never go away and never leave me all alone, ever, ever again?

"Do you love me?" Waiting, listening for the response.

"Yes," Bernie said. "I love you, Tracy. I love you."

And then the grin, through the tears, the utter relief, finally hearing what she needed so badly to hear. "Good," she said. "I love you, too." And she was in his arms, hugging, both of them crying, and all I could think about was the so many times throughout my childhood, knowing they loved my brother more, but never being able to ask or to hear the answer when it was given. I hoped Tracy would be able to hear it.

"Puke-city!" said Mike from his perch on the couch.

"Do you love me, do you love me," mimicked Joe, mincing around the room while even Franklin began to giggle. And soon they all took up the crazy, squeaky chant: do you love me, do you love me, and Paul, catching the energy, began twirling around the room, stripping off one article of clothing after another, and Corinne did her butterfly dance and James went off to stare at the light socket, and that was that. I dried my tears and took the boys out to play basketball, and once again Tracy and I became strangers.

That night, as I lay in bed, exhausted, I fell into a memory I hadn't had in years, of myself as a little girl in the front seat of a car, next to my father, driving in the dark, my mother and brother asleep in the back. So easy to pretend, I remembered, only me and my father all alone in the whole wide world, grown-up, special, my daddy's only girl in the forbidden magic of the darkness. I watched the hypnotic steadiness of the bright headlights as they softly straightened the curves, like my mother's hands smoothing the wrinkles from the sheets on the big bed. But these were my father's hands guiding the wheel, big hands with thick, dark hair growing up way past the knuckles, almost to the fingernail, and back the other way, far up under the cuffs of the blue jacket he wore. They scared me sometimes, these hands, but that night they looked gentle, relaxed, as they rested on the wheel, turning, keeping me safe. I remembered feeling the stillness like a sheet, floating down over me as I wriggled a little bit on the seat and then was still as my father began to sing, softly, in his deep baritone, who killed cock robin, and wanting to cry because it was so sad, poor cock robin, only not so much sad as sweet and bewildering, as I realized with a stab of jealousy that it was not to me he sang, and that Mommy would wake up soon. But over the bitterness came the unspoken love in the stillness, spreading inside and welling up in my heart and eyes, splashing silent tears past a tight throat in the dark. "Who saw him die, I said the fly, with my little eye, I saw him die

. . . all the birds in the air fell a sighin' and a sobbin' when they heard of the death of poor cock robin." Softly, softly—so as not to wake the others, I realized—and I soaked the love up all to myself, love spreading out like tendrils from soul to soul, touching without words like the breeze blowing against my cheek, like a huge womb, gently bobbing in the warmth all together and oh so safe, all the birds in the air . . . a sighin' and a sobbin' . . . the lilting rhythm of waves lapping on the hot sand, lulling me, too, to sleep in the darkness.

In the morning I woke up feeling that I knew the answer, had found the words that alone could save Tracy, and that I had to tell her before it was too late. But at breakfast Tracy was angry again and took an egg and threw it at Franklin and was sent to her room until she could behave.

Lee

"Don't sit there!" he screamed. I jumped back.

"Why not?" I asked.

He laughed. "Are you crazy?"

Baffled, I turned to Bernie, who was standing by the counter, spreading peanut butter onto rows of whole wheat bread and trying to keep Paul's fingers out of the jar.

"It's his men," Bernie said.

"What?"

"The little green men. They seem to be following him around today, don't they, Lee?"

"Uh-huh," Lee said, brushing off the bench with the back of his hand. "Okay. Now you can sit there," he said. So I sat.

"Hey, Bernie," he said. "Are you making sandwiches for my people?"

"Nope," Bernie said. "You're just going to have to share yours with them, I guess."

"Oh, well, that's okay. I don't think they like peanut butter, anyway." With a tremendous sense of déjà vu, I remembered this same scene being played out in our own kitchen, at home, between my mother and little brother. His men liked cookies, I recalled. But my brother had been four at the time, and Lee was fifteen, a head taller than I. He had a chunky, solid build which made him look even older, despite his boyish round face. His eyes were light grey and sunk deep in their sockets. The flesh around them was puffy, giving him a perpetually sleepy, sluggish expression.

"Jesus Christ, Lee," Tracy said, sitting down across the table. "How come you get crazier and crazier every day? I thought this place was supposed to make you less nuts, not more . . ."

"Enough, Trace," said Lois.

I had been at the RTC only three weeks, and as so often in these early days, I felt confused, out of my depth. Lee had seemed one of the saner ones around. He neither rocked aimlessly like Paul, hurt himself like Corinne, stared into light sockets, laughing, like James, nor peed in his room, like Tracy. He had even written a play, a few nights before, about a boy who rescued his mother from a boating accident; we had spent an evening in rehearsal with Lee starring as the boy, and Joan playing the mother, until Lee got fed up with our thespian shortcomings and stomped off to his room in disgust. I had noticed his insecurity, of course: he would often stop me in the middle of an activity and ask me if I liked him, if I thought he were smart, if his play were really good. But I saw nothing particularly insane about that. I had even asked Bernie, his primary, what he was doing at the RTC. Bernie answered bitterly that Lee was severely depressed yet unable to acknowledge that fact. A year ago he had consumed a bottle of his mother's sleeping pills and eaten an entire box of her chocolate laxative candies. His mother, in an alcoholic stupor, was glad he was being so quiet for a change, and he would probably have died had he not panicked and called the hospital himself before he passed out.

After that, I watched Lee more closely. I noticed that he both moved and talked like someone underwater, as if both cost him a tremendous effort. His voice had the garbled, toneless quality of a record on too slow a speed. Indeed, all of his actions were lethargic. When I thought about it later, I realized that the strangest thing about him was that he seemed devoid of emotion—almost too sane. He had, I thought, literally *depressed* his ability to feel, and for the first time I felt that I understood the meaning of the term. I never saw him admit to being sad or happy or angry or scared or loving or hating. He complained often of being bored. But somehow I had convinced myself that he was basically a "normal" kid. Hallucinations, to me, were another issue altogether. I wondered if Lee really was getting "crazier," or if maybe he was just faking, trying to get attention.

"You know, Mr. Lee," said Lois, obviously thinking the same thing, "your court hearing's coming up in a few days."

"So?"

"So, how do you think the judge is going to feel about sending someone home when they're being followed by little green men?"

No bite. "That's okay. They'll come home with me. They can keep me company, so I don't get lonely again when my mom goes out."

"What do you think you'll do if you do feel lonely?"

"But I won't be, not with all these guys around."

"Well, what will you do if they go back to wherever they

came from? After all, they haven't been around all that long. How do you know they'll stay?"

Lee took a bite of the sandwich Bernie had placed in front of him. He answered, his voice muffled further by the peanut butter. "Oh, they'll stay. They like me. We're friends."

The farm kids, who had stopped on their way over from the schoolroom for a brief basketball game, filed into the kitchen and ended the impromptu therapy session.

"Where, where, where do they come from?" asked Peter, sliding onto the bench next to Tracy.

"Ugh! You stink!" she said.

"You are asking for a time out, dear," Lois said to Tracy, gesturing toward the corner of the room where the kids were made to stand when they refused to cooperate or were unable to control themselves. "This is a warning."

"Where do they come from, Lee?" Peter went on. "Would it be good if everyone had some? Would it be good? Would it be good if everyone had lit—"

"Whatcha got, Lee?" asked Alex, bouncing a basketball in the doorway.

"Just forget it."

"Cigs?"

"I said, forget it."

"Jesus Christ, I was just asking! Hey, Bernie, what's for lunch?"

"What, what, what's for lunch, Bernie?" Peter chimed in.

"Lee's seeing martians or something," said Tracy. "But then, he's crazy."

"Fuck you. Whore."

"Hey Bernie, did you hear what Lee—"

"One more word out of anyone and we're going to spend the entire afternoon doing math problems. No park, no basketball, no nothing. So just keep it up."

Still the "new one," I felt again awkward and unsure, less a staffer than a slightly saner friend, and sometimes not even that. I tried to start a conversation with James, sitting on my left, but Peter kept breaking in with incessant and insistent questions about whether I liked peanut butter, and whether it would be good if everyone in the world liked peanut butter, or only ate peanut butter, or whether I would like it if all the peanut butter in the world were right there in the kitchen, and whether that would be good, and Lee kept wanting to know if I knew how to play backgammon, and whether I would play some with him that evening, after the farm kids had gone home, he said, glaring at Peter, and Alex kept trying to spit on Tracy's sandwich, and telling Lee he was glad that at least he had a home to go to, a farm, and that was sure better than staying here with a bunch of crazies, he said, staring at Paul, who was rocking in the corner, clutching his favorite, clothbound *Rudolph the Red-Nosed Reindeer* book to his chest. And James sat too, laughing softly into his sandwich, until I gave up.

Lee cornered me after dinner. "Wanna play backgammon?" he asked.

"Sure," I said.

He got the set from the playroom, and we laid it out on the kitchen table. "I want to be whites," he said.

"Okay." He lined his pieces up carefully, straightening the rows with his fingers. "I go first," he said, tossing his dice into the cup and shaking vigorously. A six and a three. He frowned, then slid his pieces slowly along the board. I picked up my dice.

"So what do you think of this place?" he asked.

Double sixes. Shit. On the very first move. What must he think, I thought. Normally I had terrible luck in board games.

"Jesus, you're lucky, huh?" he said.

"Sometimes." I wondered whether I should let him win or whether that would be too obvious. I decided that I'd better at least make a show of trying, and moved my pieces down the board.

"I don't know," I said. "I haven't really been here long enough to tell." He had rolled a four and a two and smiled, doubling up his pieces. "What do you think of it?"

"Oh," he said, his voice flat. "It's all right, I guess. I mean, if you're crazy and you need it and all. I needed it when I first came, I guess, but now that I'm better, it seems pretty boring." He paused. "I guess that means I'm ready to go home, huh?"

I rolled and moved, barely concentrating, again wondering what I should say, why every conversation with these kids turned so quickly into a minefield, why the rest of the staff even trusted me alone with the kids. Jason had cautioned me briefly to steer clear of explosive topics, at least at first. Try and keep it neutral, he said, and I remembered seeing that word on a page in some psych textbook, pictured myself reading the page in the science library on a sunny fall day when I would much rather have been outside.

"I don't know," I said. "How do you feel about going home?" Oh, God, I thought. I can't believe I said that with a straight face. I sounded like a parody of a high school guidance counselor and I knew it. At least I have the good sense to be embarrassed, I thought. I expected him to laugh in my face.

He seemed to think it a perfectly reasonable question. "Well, I want to, of course. I want to be with my mom." He shook the dice. "I'm really all she's got. She needs me. And, you know, this place does get pretty boring." He rolled. Double fours. "Ha! You're in trouble now," he said.

I thought back to what Bernie had told me over drinks the night before—that Lee's mother, an alcoholic who lived with her son in a two-room trailer in the predominantly Indian town of Pontilla had, in the year since Lee had been at the center, consistently refused to either visit or call her son, despite frequent requests by the staff that she do so. Indeed, her inability to provide emotional support for him, her utter lack of interest in his well-being coupled with an alcoholic seductiveness that preyed on his adolescent imagination, was probably the main reason for his attempted suicide one year before.

I rolled. "Well," I said, moving my pieces without even noticing where they landed, "doesn't home ever get sort of boring too?"

His voice took on a grating edge. "Naah. Not really. Not like here. Me and my mom, we do stuff . . . and my friends . . ." Pale, freckled Lee, the whitey, the gringo, whose body still bore scars of the well-aimed rocks his "friends" had thrown. "*You* know," he said, picking up the dice. He rolled, a two and a one. "How come I never get the good rolls?" he whined.

"Don't worry," I said. "Luck always evens out in the end." I rolled. Double fives. Oh, great, I thought. Lee scowled.

"This game is boring," he said. "I like playing with Bernie better than you."

"Why?"

"I don't know. I just do." He picked up the dice again.

"I got winners!" Tracy said, sliding in next to me on the bench.

Lee frowned at her. "Can you please leave us alone?" he said. "We're talking."

"You can't kick me out of the kitchen. I have just as much right to be here as you do. If you want to talk, go into your bedroom."

"Liz, ask her to leave . . ."

"Well . . ."

Lee lunged across the table and shoved Tracy off the bench, knocking most of the backgammon pieces onto the floor.

"I said, get out!" he yelled, and then "Oh, forget it," and he stormed out of the room, leaving Tracy in a tangled heap on the floor and me standing there with no idea of what to do next, except that, somehow, I couldn't let Lee off so easy.

Richard, another staff member, came in. "What happened here?" he said.

"Oh, Lee kind of lost it, I guess." I helped Tracy to her feet.

"Yeah. Asshole," she said.

After looking at her to make sure she was okay, Richard sent her into the TV room and took me aside, patiently explaining to me things I immediately felt I should have realized on my own—how upset Lee was at the threat of leaving, how scared he was of his court hearing later that week, how angry he was at his mother for her steadfast refusal to say that she wanted him back, and how important it was for him that we all be understanding, that we show him it was all right for him to need to stay awhile longer, to show him that no, he was not yet well enough to go home and survive.

Then he looked at my face, the hot, ashamed flush burning my cheeks. "It's not as much of a disaster as you think," he said, his crisp Australian voice becoming soft and his blue eyes a little less intense. "Actually, he needs to get mad. He doesn't do that often enough, really." He laughed. "You've got to stop thinking that one false move from you is going to send them over the edge. All of these kids have survived a lot—things that would probably have killed you or me. One little screw-up from a well meaning but basically inconsequential person is hardly going to do it."

I smiled, at the same time feeling stung by his easy dismissal of me as inconsequential. Sure, I didn't want the responsibility of having the power to upset another person's mind, but I did very much want to see myself as healer, as making the difference. All the glory, none of the pain, I told myself. I felt the flush in my cheeks deepen as I dug my fingernails into my palm. Idiot, I told myself.

"I do think, though," he said, "that you should go talk to him."

"What do you think I should say?" I asked, still looking at the floor.

"I don't know. Why don't you just see whether you can get him to tell you what happened."

Oh sure, I thought, walking slowly down the hall to the room Lee shared with Paul. Nothing to it.

Lee was lying on his bed, his muddy boots resting on the plaid bedspread. He jiggled one foot back and forth as he lay on his back, flipping the pages of a comic book. I could not see his face. "Can I come in?" I asked.

"Sure," he said, without looking up. His voice was flat. "Sorry about the game. I guess I just got bored of playing. I hope you don't mind. You can always play with Tracy, you know, if you want . . ."

"It's okay if you don't feel like playing," I said, "but I think it would have been better if you'd just told me, instead of taking it out on Tracy."

He put down the comic and looked at me for the first time. His eyes were wide open, the lashes obscured by the puffiness of his brow. I could not tell what he was thinking. "What are you talking about?" he asked.

"I'm talking about you pushing Tracy off the bench."

He sighed, and when he spoke, his voice was even, condescending. He was explaining an obvious point to a slow child, and he did not relish the task. "I didn't push her. She fell. She's always trying to get attention like that."

"Lee, I saw you. You pushed her."

His face took on a pained expression, and he picked up the comic book again. "Oh, sure," he said. "I just jumped up and attacked her for no reason. Fine." His voice was soft. He was humoring me. "Come on, Liz. You know I don't get angry. Just ask Bernie, he'll tell you. Of course, you can believe whatever you want. But we both know the truth. It's okay, though. I knew you would take her side. You women are all alike. You always stick together. I can't wait till I get out of here." He flopped back on the bed and began to read.

I could not tell whether he was lying, trying to escape a punishment I was not going to mete out, or whether he really did not remember or did not understand what he had done. Or maybe she really had fallen, I thought. I tried to play back the scene in my mind and suddenly was unsure. I felt as if I were the crazy one. "I'm not mad at you," I said, hoping to coax an admission of guilt. "I can understand that you got angry at her for interrupting our game, and at me for letting her—"

"I'm not angry," he said. "Why should I be? I was just tired of playing, that's all."

"But—"

"Look," he said, putting the comic book down once more. "I've got a lot on my mind right now, okay? My court hearing's coming up in a couple of days. Otherwise I'd be happy to play with you. But right now I'd just like to be alone. Okay?"

I was dumbfounded, absolutely stumped. I smiled stupidly, wondering what I was supposed to do. Should I yell at him? Tell him he was nuts? I wanted to run and ask Richard, but knew that as soon as I left the room, with Lee in control, the opportunity would be lost.

"You know," I said finally, "I'm sorry I didn't just tell Tracy to get out of the kitchen. We were talking, and it was rude of her to interrupt like that. And wrong of me to let her." I checked his face for any sign of a reaction, but there was none. Still, at least he was listening. "I know you're scared about your hearing, and—"

"Scared?" he said. "Are you kidding? The judge will believe I'm sane, even if you guys don't. You're the one who's crazy, not me. I can't wait to get out of here."

"All right," I said. "But—"

"Could I please be alone now?" he asked. "I really just need some space." I smiled, marveling at how good these kids were at quoting our psych scriptures for their own purposes.

"Okay," I said at last. "But let's talk some more later. Okay?"

"Yeah. Sure."

I left the room, realizing only after I saw Tracy's angry scowl that Lee had managed to get off easy, after all.

At breakfast the next day, Lee was as whiny as ever, his voice the same monotone and his conversation the same litany of complaints and fantasies. Even his little green men had disappeared, I found, when I sat down next to him abruptly—or perhaps they just weren't attending breakfast that morning. At noon, his lawyer came to take him out to lunch in town, and he seemed cheerful enough when he got back. He even asked me for a game of backgammon, which we played without incident, my lucky streak of the previous day having vanished. "Good game," he said, triumphantly tossing the last of his pieces into the box. He didn't even seem upset when Tracy stepped in to play "losers."

During the staff meeting that afternoon, we discussed what we should do about him, how we could persuade him to stay at the center a while longer, and how we could tell him that we didn't think he was ready to go home without ensuring his failure if he decided (and was allowed by the judge) to go anyway. That is, *they* discussed it, tossing their opinions about as easily as if he'd been a new advertising campaign or a character in a movie. They talked as I sat there listening with the intrigued, slightly guilty feeling I remembered from nights when I would sit up past my bedtime in the living room when my parents had a dinner party, listening to the grownups talk about things I knew I shouldn't be hearing, keeping myself still and silent for fear that someone would notice me and remember I should be in bed.

I studied them as the talk went around the room, wondering as I looked at them all, so different, lounging comfortably in the soft furniture, what had brought them all here. Jason spoke first, his large body sprawled in a corner of the couch, his voice, as always, surprisingly soft and smooth. I had heard him tell Alex a few days before that he, like Alex, had also thought it would be fun to kill someone, and had signed up to go to the Vietnam war before he was drafted. Yes, he had told Alex, his southern drawl flat and quiet, he had killed some gooks, and had seen his best friends get killed as well. It wasn't fun, he said, and Alex had listened, unconvinced. Jason had come home and vowed never again to cut his hair. Its smooth golden waves flowed down over his broad shoulders. Of all the staff, I found Jason the most reassuring, the one I would want to have comfort me if anything ever went wrong. He was a large man, with huge hands that could palm a basketball or grasp the flailing arms of a child out of control. There was a solidness about him, a three-dimensional being in a world of shadows. He reminded me of an oak tree in a grove of willows: tall, solid, stable, something to cling to when the gale got too strong. He felt we should be honest with Lee, that he deserved at least that much from us, and that lying wouldn't help in the long run, anyway.

Bernie disagreed. He sat at the other end of the couch from Jason, his hard, narrow body leaning forward over his bony knees, his foot, in a worn blue Addidas sneaker, tapping restlessly on the rug. Bernie was never still. Where Jason soothed, Bernie liked to stir the kids up, make them laugh, show them in a million subtle ways that he was as "crazy" as they, that the distance between them was less than they thought, that they, too, could make it if they tried. If Jason was a rock for them to cling to, Bernie was the siren on the rock, beckoning, dancing. His grey eyes rolled to the ceiling. "What exactly did you have in mind?" he asked Jason.

"I just think that at the very least we should tell him that we're going to ask the judge for another six months. And why."

"Oh, great," Bernie said. "Let's tell him he's nuts so that when the judge does let him go home, and face it, you know she will—"

Lois snorted. She clutched her coffee cup with one hand

and gestured with the other, pointing her burning cigarette at Bernie, across the room. "Oh? Just because the judge is a woman you think—"

"He can really lose it," Bernie continued.

Richard, the tough Aussie from the outback whom I found unpredictable, took Jason's side. And so they argued back and forth, each with his own philosophies and hurts and love for the kids, and in the end they decided to tell Lee the truth, and hope that they could persuade him to stay.

The job of telling him fell to Bernie, his primary. And so Bernie told him, he told me later that night when we were together in the quiet kitchen, after all the kids had gone to bed. Told him that couldn't he see that he was much better off here with us, with people who cared about him and took care of him and gave him presents for his birthday (when was the last time your mother called you up, Lee? When was the last time she gave you a party on your birthday? Do you really think she cares?) as Lee sat there, his muscles tensed, glaring at Bernie with all the suppressed rage in his soul, saying it was only money, that she didn't have the money to do all that stuff, it wasn't her fault and she would if she could, as Bernie asked quietly how much she spent on liquor a month, until Lee finally told him to fuck off, that he was well now, she needed him, he could make it all better, all problems gone. Could and should. And would. "But what about the little green men?" Bernie asked.

"I was just making them up," Lee said, staring at the bedspread next to him. "I knew they were fake. I was just bullshitting you."

"Okay," said Bernie. Then he slammed his hand down hard on the spot on which Lee's eyes were fastened and watched the boy wince and mouth "Don't!" "Sure, you were just making them up." Until finally Lee began to cry, and say he was sorry, that he didn't want to go, he wanted to stay, that Bernie was right, he was happier here, he couldn't make it there, he was scared, he wanted to stay.

"And so I hugged him," Bernie said to me. "Told him I was glad, and that I thought he was doing the right thing. And that was that."

And that was that. Except that the next day, in court, Lee, looking spiffy and sane in his brand-new tie and navy blazer, told the judge that he wanted more than anything to go home.

". . . both auditory and visual hallucinations . . ." Bernie was saying. "Unprovoked attack against a girl at the center just two days ago. Depressed. Not ready to go home. Needs another six months . . . "

And Lee, calm and condescending, said, "Not hallucinations, just kidding. I know they weren't real. Not depressed, just bored. Didn't attack her, playing . . . "

I watched the judge listen, taking it all in, obviously thinking that this serious and rational and effortlessly calm child should be home, with his mother (who did not, it was noted by Bernie, attend the hearing, even though the center had offered to pay her bus fare all the way from Pontilla and back again) who loved him. She was a mother, too, the judge said. And when, in answer to Bernie's reiteration that Lee's mother failed even to notice his birthday, Lee said that "all he wanted for his birthday was his mother's love," we saw the judge's eyes cloud over with tears, and we knew that we had just lost and that Lee, in his deluded and frightened pride, had won. And we were right.

"Released to the custody of his mother," the judge said. And that really was that.

Lee was triumphant as he left the courtroom, gloating to the staff that he knew all along that the judge would be able to see that he was sane, even if we were too dumb to notice, and accepting the envious congratulations of the other kids with muted pride and smiles of assurance.

Bernie and I drove him to Pontilla the next day. As the mountains receded, the sky appeared enormous, opening out over the snow-covered plains like a vast blue umbrella. Horses shivered in their pastures in the biting wind, and Lee edged closer to me on the seat. His smile had faded.

"Will you write to me?" he asked.

"Of course we will," Bernie said. "But that means you'd better learn how to read."

Lee flushed angrily. "I know how to read. Just make sure you remember how to write." He slammed his body backward in the seat and glared at Bernie. But soon his body softened again. He stared out the window, watching the sagebrush blur by on the right, their branches encased in ice, sagging under their own weight. Then he turned to Bernie. His eyes looked vacant. "Do you think I can come visit sometimes?"

Bernie reached over and slapped him on the leg. "I thought you couldn't wait to get out."

"I couldn't wait not to live there," he explained, "but I might like to come just for a little while sometime . . . see how the kids are doing and all. You know."

"Well, I don't know." Bernie said. "We'll see. I'm not sure what kind of influence you'd be. On the kids, that is. Like you said before, they're gonna be mighty jealous of you. What makes you think they'll want to see you?"

Lee bit his lip, and I decided that Bernie was carrying

his tough-guy act too far. "Of course you can visit," I said. "We want you to. We'll miss you, kiddo."

Lee looked at Bernie. "Will you?"

"Of course we will," Bernie said. "I mean, with you gone, who's going to lose to me at backgammon?"

Lee looked out the window again. "I'll miss you, too," he told the sagebrush. He rubbed his thumb against his nose, and then let it rest against his lips. I watched him as he stared out the window, first licking his thumb with short jabs of his tongue, and then slowly allowing it to slide inside his mouth. My chest hurt; I was finding it difficult to breathe.

"It'll be okay," I said, putting my hand on Lee's shoulder. "And if it's not, you just give us a call, and we'll try to work it out. Okay?" But he didn't turn around. I did not know whether he had heard me or not.

We got off the highway at Pontilla, and drove through the town as Lee mumbled unclear directions. Neon signs lit up either side of the main road: Speedy's Motor Inn, McDonald's, Dairy Queen, Burger King, the Saints and Sinners Bar, and on and on, lining the road. Cars whizzed by, drag racing up and down this main strip, their chassis an inch off the ground.

"*Cholos,*" Lee said.

"What?"

"Low riders. They think they're hot shit."

"Happy to be home, Lee?" Bernie asked.

"Shut up," Lee said. And then, "Turn left at the light. Here!" He leaned forward, and, for the first time, he did look happy to be home.

He directed us through streets of small ranch houses with dozens of small dirty children playing outside. "Honkys!"

they jeered, seeing our van. There was not one white face.

Finally we pulled into a trailer park, row after row of small, narrow trailers set up in careful grids. "This is it," Lee said, and we pulled up in front of a pink mobile home. The outside was streaked with dirt and grease, and it looked dark. Forbidding.

But to Lee, it was home again, and he jumped out of the van and ran inside. The screen door banged shut after him then flew open again, swaying on its hinges. We followed, uncertain.

I stood in the doorway, blinking my eyes to adjust to the gloom. As the forms began to come into focus, I saw that we were standing in the kitchen. Dirty dishes were piled in the sink, the overflow resting on the adjoining counter. Cockroaches feasted from half-eaten jars of Libby's potted meat product, Vienna sausages and Spaghetti-Os that lay on the kitchen table, along with a package of Saltines. From where we stood, I could see the living room. A battered couch slumped against one wall, its faded fabric buried under piles of stained undershirts and socks. Jagged metal coils poked out from the cushions, glinting silver in the crevices. A few feet away, a coffee table, sticky with grape jelly dripping from a plastic spoon, held ashtrays that overflowed onto the floor. Half-smoked cigarettes and broken pretzel sticks were ground into the olive green carpet like dead bugs. On another wall, a poster of two sailboats, spinnakers soaring, hung between two closed windows, which were covered by torn white shades. Two scrawny orange cats fought in a corner. The odor of cat excrement filled the air.

A black and white portable television flickered soundlessly on the kitchen table. Seated in front of it was a large woman. She did not appear to be watching, but clutched a beer, sipping it occasionally and then letting it rest against her lower lip as she sucked on the rim. She wore a loose-fitting floral print blouse and orange stretch pants, and her face was smeared with make-up. Sparkly blue shadow glittered on her closed lids.

Lee went to her, touching her shoulder gently with his hand and leaning down to kiss her face. "Hi, mom," he said.

The woman opened her eyes with an effort, and smiled. "Hello, son!" she boomed. "Welcome home."

Katie

One year after Katie came to the center, she burned the place down. Furious one night at Lois, her primary, for keeping her home from the movies, she set fire to the drapes in her room, left, and then calmly asked to be taken for a walk. By the time they got back, the house was in flames, and by the time the firemen arrived, the house had burned to the ground. Katie was thrilled to be at the center of such bright-red, masculine attention, and when the other kids returned, Katie gloated to them, laughing because they had missed the excitement.

Of course, it didn't take anyone long to figure out what had happened. Indeed, once the enormity of what she had done became real to her, Katie confessed easily. But it is one thing to punish a child for swearing or not making her bed. How do you punish a crazy girl for burning down the house? You can't and they didn't. Rather, they set about deciding what to do next.

For two weeks or so, they all moved up the road into the guest house, which Dan Johnson generally used for visiting dignitaries or relatives, or as a retreat for his own family when things got out of hand up at the farm where they lived. The kids loved the luxury of the place: two television sets, a real kitchen, as they put it, with food in the cabinets and not all locked up in the pantry, carpeting on the floor, and a host of other amenities. But the novelty soon wore off, and the reality remained that seven crazy children could not coexist peacefully in a two-bedroom house.

So they began to farm the kids out. James, tall, frail, schizophrenic, went to live with a carpenter down the road, who set him to work making adobe bricks, sawing wood and pouring cement. A kind German couple in the valley took in Paul and Corinne, autistic brother and sister, and lavished on them all the love they had given to their own daughter, who had died the year before. Katie, Tracy and the rest of the kids who were there at the time all went up to the farm to live, where they were teased and tortured by the farm children with varying degrees of cruelty, and where they adjusted with varying degrees of success. The RTC staff found themselves pretty much out of a job for the summer, except for helping out up at the farm when they were needed.

The house burned down in the beginning of June, and by mid-August the new house, made of nonflammable adobe and specially treated wood, was finished. James ended his job with the carpenter, his sanity vanishing as soon as it was no longer needed.

"No," Jason said, interrupting Richard, who was telling

me the story one evening. Jason explained that James was like a deciduous tree, shedding his sanity like leaves each fall and having it blossom in the spring, only to fade away again as summer melted into October.

"Whatever," Richard said.

To everyone's astonishment, the German couple fell in love with Paul, and announced that they wanted to adopt him—although not Corinne. Paul himself seemed happier, calmer, slightly less filled with rage. He still did not talk, but his eye contact was better, and he had begun to approach the people he trusted and physically ask for caresses by stroking a forearm. Jason and Lois were thrilled, of course, and immediately set the legal machinery in motion. Then, the husband, a military attaché, got transferred overseas. Or maybe his mother got sick, Richard said, I really don't remember. But whatever, they had to leave the United States and, moreover, the woman had herself become pregnant with their own child. As much as it broke their hearts, they had to tell Dan Johnson that they could no longer manage to adopt the child. So Paul, too, came back to live in his brand-new adobe prison.

Tracy came back from the farm furious and resentful. She could not understand why she had been made to return to the RTC, when two of the other children had been allowed to stay at the farm. "What's the matter," she had asked. "Am I too crazy to stay up there, is that it?" And what the fuck did they think she was going to do up there anyway, that was so horrible? Run away? She could run away from the RTC, too, she said, and she would, in a second, if they tried to make her stay. But the staff knew the truth, that Tracy was still too sick to make it up at the farm. She, more than any of the other kids, needed the security of knowing there were people around to control her when she was unable to control herself. She still needed the freedom to be crazy, to scream and curse and hurl herself in fury against Jason's bulk, to act out the rage she had not yet learned to express in words. The staff did the best they could. In vain they pointed out to her that she hadn't been very happy at the farm, that the other kids hadn't been very nice, that at the RTC she could have all the extra attention she wanted, and finally that they would have missed her too much up at the farm, so she needed to come back and keep them company. She was not fooled.

Katie, on the other hand, came back to the center a changed person. Before the fire, Richard said, Katie had channeled all her energies into denying the beginnings of her sexuality. With every ounce of strength in her soul, she had struggled to turn back the clock. Before the fire, she would spend hours curled in a fetal position against Lois's warm back, sucking on a bottle filled with milk. Being asked to go to school, or dress herself, or even cut her own meat at dinner would produce screaming tantrums that could last for days. She refused to do anything a baby could not do: she refused to walk, she could not, she said, and so crawled from place to place. She refused to, or no longer could, exercise bowel and bladder control and insisted on being dressed in diapers under her skirts. She could speak only a few words: "mama," by which she addressed Lois, "dada," which she called all the men at the RTC, "milk," "bottle," "doggie," "yes," and, most often, "no." Slowly, as the year before the fire wore on, she had begun to allow herself to regain some measure of independence, but her conversations still consisted of baby talk, and her rages were still mute tantrums.

With the fire, Richard said, most of these symptoms had gone, literally, up in smoke. Somehow, setting the fire had allowed her to vent the rage she felt at having been trapped for her thirteen years in a family in which, every Monday and Thursday night, her father would make a late-night pilgrimage to her room, crawl under the covers beside her, and rape her through her tears.

"But didn't she tell anyone?" I asked.

Oh yes, Richard said, she had of course told her mother, way back in the beginning when she was about ten, but her mother hadn't believed her, had said, in fact, looking at her daughter's blossoming breasts and widening hips, that it was all just Katie's wish, to steal her father from his wife and have him all to herself, and that if Katie didn't stop behaving so seductively, and telling such ridiculous lies, she would personally take her to the doctor and have her sterilized.

It was then that Katie had begun her unsuccessful campaign to run away from home. Sometimes she would last weeks, sometimes only days, but in the end she was always found and returned home by a policeman. After the fourth or fifth time, her mother decided that enough was enough and that she had not been put on this earth to spend her life searching for an ungrateful bitch, even if the bitch happened to be her daughter. So Katie was sent to us.

Katie had begun and ended her career as an arsonist the summer before I arrived, and the story was told to me by way of introduction the day before she returned to the RTC from a week-long visit with her prospective adoptive parents. Certainly Richard was right: some good had come out of the fire, because the girl I met in the kitchen that day bore no relation to the deeply disturbed, regressive adolescent of whom he had spoken.

When I met her, Katie was a cheerful, albeit immature fourteen-year-old. She had a soft, chubby body with large, rounded breasts and wide hips, which she hid under flowing blouses and loose slacks. She stood awkwardly, her arms often folded across her chest, as if to hide the femininity beneath. The maturity of her body contrasted strangely with the childish expression on her round face. She usually held her chapped red lips pursed in a clownish smile, and her large brown eyes open wide, in contrast to the tight, hostile demeanor of the other kids at the center. She wore no makeup, and her forehead and chin were covered with acne, the red dots standing out against her pale skin. Considering her history, I found her remarkably trusting. She seemed in constant need of physical affection, as though tactile love was the only kind of which she could be sure, and she often rubbed up against the staff, both male and female. Her friendliness and need to be liked were apparent in every movement.

"Hewwo, Wois," she crooned, as she bounded through the front door.

"Hi, Kate!" Lois said, giving her a hug. "No baby talk now, all right?"

Katie started, then straightened up, nodding obediently. Looking around, she noticed me. "Who's that?"

"Why don't you ask her?" Lois said.

Having ascertained my name, Katie gave me a wide-open smile and came to sit next to me, her leg pressed up against mine. She told me about the Robertsons, the amazing family—as she said, her mom, her dad, and her brothers—who had actually chosen, out of all the kids in the whole wide world, to adopt *her*.

"That's wonderful," I said, and she threw her arms around me in a big hug.

Tracy came into the kitchen, a sullen look on her face. "Hi," she said, not looking at Katie. She snuggled up to me on my other side. "Can you play with me?"

Katie glared at Tracy. "Can't you see I'm talking to her?"

"She doesn't want to be your friend," said Tracy. "You're leaving in a couple of months, anyway. She's here for me."

I looked at them both. They were almost exactly the same size and shape, both chunky, round, both larger than I, both with ragged hair that hung down over their foreheads in sharp spikes. They were the same age, too, and had suffered many of the same traumas. Yet they were completely different. Where Tracy was dark and sullen and hard, Katie was malleable. Where Tracy was strong and angry, Katie was tractable. And now Katie had added the largest difference of all. She was wanted. And Tracy was not.

Trying to be fair, I moved both of them gently away, and explained that I was there for everyone, that if Katie were only going to be around for a little while then that was all the more reason I should get to know her now, as there would be plenty of time to be with Tracy in the months to come.

As soon as I'd finished my speech I knew I'd said the wrong thing but it was too late. As far as Tracy was concerned, I could have been a judge handing down a life sentence. "Fine. Be that way. Bitch," she screamed, running from the room.

Katie looked smug. "If she doesn't stop cursing and losing control, she's never gonna find anyone to adopt her. Right, Lois?"

"It's easy for you to talk now, missy," said Lois. "But let's not forget that it isn't a very long time since you—"

"Okay, okay." Katie cut her off. Then she smiled again. Her crooked, discolored teeth jutted forward in her round face. Lois and I both smiled back at her eagerness, and her smile widened still further in a reflection of ours. "Can I help you give Corey her bath?" she asked. "Mom said I might be able to help sometimes with my little brother, so I need to learn how."

I marveled at how easily, even eagerly, she used those words: mom, brother, dad, to refer to a family of relative strangers, when she had been taken from her real mom, dad, and brothers little more than a year before. In her own mind, she had erased her first family, the one that had hurt her, and was now trying as hard as she could to replace them with the new. Her desire to forget was so overpowering, and her need to make her new family part of her history as well as her future so enormous, that I grew used to hearing her delve into or fabricate a childhood memory that included the adoptive family rather than her real one. "When I was little, my mom and I used to . . . " she would say, and mean her adoptive mother rather than her biological one. The staff discouraged her rewriting of history in this way, insisting that it was important to understand and acknowledge the bad of the old as well as the good of the new. But I sat there that afternoon, watching her bathe Corinne who lay submerged in the water, happily playing like a small pink whale. I saw how gentle, almost maternal Katie's caresses were as she ran the soapy washcloth over Corinne's arms and played "this little piggy" with her toes, as Corinne squealed and splashed in the tub. And I found myself hoping that Katie could erase her past pain, and live secure in the happiness of her new family. Her loving, and therefore her only real, parents.

Katie's new parents were to come and fetch her on the Monday after Easter. As Easter Sunday approached, however, Katie started to denigrate her new parents, and her conversation became riddled with references to Dan Johnson. She wanted to know if he understood how grateful she was for all he'd done; whether he knew how much she loved him; whether we thought he might adopt her as his own daughter someday; whether she shouldn't forget about her adoption and go live with him at the farm.

Dan had a firm policy against visiting the RTC—he felt, for reasons that few of the staff understood, that his presence merely served to remind the RTC kids of their "separateness." As a result, most of the kids, including Katie, had met Dan only a few times, at the annual Christmas dinner, or at their initial screenings. Because he was so remote, Dan took on mythic proportions for many of the kids. They knew him only as their savior; through his largesse, they had come to be happier, safer, saner. All of the kids wished to be his child at one time or another. But to Katie this wish became an obsession. "He came the night of the fire," she reminded us constantly. "He could'a really killed me that night. But he didn't. He didn't even yell at me or anything. He didn't even get mad. I guess he must really like me, huh?"

We all tried to discourage her fantasies and to talk to her instead of the new life she was about to embark on. We spent hours role-playing with her, coaching her through family arguments and new-school situations, through bus routes and supermarkets and through saying no to sex and drugs. At the end of each session, though, Katie would caution, "That is, if Dan doesn't adopt me first."

Finally, Lois decided that Katie needed to confront reality in the person of Dan himself. "Why don't you make Dan a present?" Lois said one afternoon. "You can give it to him when you say good-bye. That way, he'll always have something that will make him think of you, even after you're with your new family."

"But what could I make?" Katie moaned. "I can't do anything . . . "

Jason rubbed her back. "Sure you can, babe. You could paint him a picture, or make an ashtray . . . the point is, it'd be from you. That's the important thing."

Katie was convinced. For the next few days, she poured her being into a lumpy clay ashtray. Over and over she molded it, smashing the fruits of an afternoon's labor in half a minute because "it isn't good enough for Dan." As she worked, she talked about where the ashtray would go, on the table, near his bed, where she would see it each night when she went to kiss him before going to sleep. Jason talked to her as she worked, trying to break into the fantasy, to remind her that she *was* being adopted, by a family with only two other kids, rather than a whole farmful, that she was loved, that she was special, but that she was being unrealistic to pin her hopes on Dan. Oh, sure, Katie would nod then, I know that, and she would laugh. But the hungry hope continued to burn in her eyes.

By the Saturday before Easter, the ashtray was finished. Lois had spoken to Dan the previous day, both to warn him and to plot a strategy. They had agreed that Katie should come up to the farm for Easter brunch, so that Dan could say good-bye to her gently, and face-to-face.

With this in mind, Lois told Katie to give Dan a call.

"But what should I say?" Katie asked. "What if he doesn't remember me? What if I can't think of anything to say? What if—"

"Just tell him you made a going-away present for him, and ask whether you can come up to the farm tomorrow and give it to him." She smiled, "Don't worry. I'm sure he'll let you come. After all, he does care about you, too. He'll want to say good-bye."

Katie still looked frightened. "Will you stay wiff me while I call?"

Katie picked up the phone and dialed the numbers that Lois gave her. On the fourth try, she got it right and we watched her clutch the phone as she listened to it ring.

"Hi," she said into the receiver. "What? Oh. This is Katie." There was a pause, and then she said. "From the RTC. Can I, uh, can I talk to D, to Dan?" More silence, and then in a loud voice she said, "Hi. This . . . is Katie. Can I . . . I want to come up and see you tomorrow."

Then she was silent. She nodded her head and bit her lip, and tears came snaking down her cheeks. "Okay," she said at last. "Good-bye." She hung up the phone and went to her room, shutting the door behind her, and would tell us nothing more about what had happened.

Dan did, though. He told Lois that he had changed his mind and decided that Katie's seeing him again would only make it harder on her when she discovered that he was not going to adopt her.

"Harder on *him,* he means," Bernie said. "He just couldn't deal with the pain up close. Really says a lot for the guy, huh?"

Jason grimaced. "What the hell did he say to her, anyway? She's a mess in there."

Well, Lois told us, Dan had simply told Katie the truth: that he cared about her, but that he could not adopt her, that he would always think of her, but that she would be better off with her own new family, a family that she could really be special to.

"Oh, great," Bernie said. "Like, with us she's just one of the crowd, but they're so pitiful that to them, she could be special."

Lois defended Dan, saying he hadn't meant it like that. "Anyway, he's right, in a way."

Richard snorted. "Sure, he's always right. Always right there, handing down orders from on high, when he doesn't know shit about these kids, and then leaves us to pick up the pieces."

"If he had let her go up there, you know she would have just gotten her hopes up. And it would have been cruel."

"Crueler than letting her spend days making a stupid ashtray that he told her to give to his secretary to bring up to the farm? Crueler than letting us allow her to believe he actually cared about her?"

Lois shrugged. She was Dan's liaison, his link between the RTC and the farm, and she was not about to say anything against him. In any case, there was nothing more to say.

The next morning, Katie came into the kitchen as usual and sat down at her place. Lois kissed her, and put a glass of milk in front of her. Katie stared at it, and then whined, "Lolo, I can't dwink from my cup. I want a ba-ba."

Lois whirled around, frightened. The Robertsons were planning to come for their new child in less than twenty-four hours. What would they do if they found an infant instead of the fourteen-year-old they were expecting? "Come on, Kate," she said. "Of course you can do it. You did it yesterday, and you can do it today. Nothing bad will happen, I promise."

"But I caaaan't," she whimpered.

Lois sat next to her. "I'll help you, sweetie," she said. She placed her hands over Katie's and helped her guide the cup to her mouth. Katie took a sip, swallowed, and smiled.

"Now you do one all by yourself," Lois said. Katie raised the cup to her lips without thinking and then, as if angered by her own strength, her own inability to hide in the insanity that had once been her best defense, she hurled it against the wall. Cold milk sprayed over the table, splashing onto the wood and Lois's hair. The cup landed in Katie's lap.

"I hate him! I hate him!" she screamed.

"Shhhhhh," Lois said. "It's okay, sweetie. It's okay."

Katie began to sob, her face collapsing as the tears and saliva dropped in slippery puddles on the table. "No, it isn't!" she shouted. "He could have adopted me, but he just didn't want to." She stopped crying as suddenly as she had started. She thrust out her lower lip, and swatted at the puddle of milk with her sleeve. "But I don't care. I'm being adopted by a real family. And who wants to live at the stupid old farm, anyway?"

Lois smiled at her. "That's the spirit," she said.

That night, during Katie's farewell party, Tracy misbehaved and was sent to her room. Alone and miserable, she filled her wastebasket with old math papers, dirty socks and three rolls of pilfered toilet paper. Then she took out a small, red book of matches that she had stolen at Katie's farewell dinner that night. She removed a single match and lit it, drinking in the sulphur smell. She watched the small yellow diamond work its way down the stem of the match, until the heat began to hurt her fingers. Carefully, she laid it down on the thinnest paper, and held her breath as it caught fire, the beautiful orange-blue flames leaping up in greeting, warming her face. When Lois found her, she was crouched on her heels, staring into the dancing colors, blowing her hot breath softly into the center to fan them. The fire was extinguished before it could do any harm.

I thought of Tracy later that night, how desperately she was searching for the magic, missing something that would make her lovable. I pictured her puzzling it out for herself: she and Katie were so alike, friends for a year because no one had wanted either of them. And then suddenly Katie was wanted. What had she found? What had changed? And then, ah, yes, Tracy must have realized. Katie had set a fire. After that, she had been wantable. They were so alike. So Tracy had set her own fire, hoping to find in its flames the secret that Katie had learned and refused to share. "I was trying to burn down the house, like Katie," Tracy had sobbed to Lois when she was discovered. But there was no miracle for her; the burning bush sputtered and went cold. Tracy gained nothing for her efforts except a furious lecture from Lois and the bone-sure knowledge that even the flames had found her wanting.

In the ensuing confusion, the anger, guilt and forgiveness, we did not have as much time to give to Katie as we would have liked. She was leaving the next day, she was frightened and we knew it, but she took it quite well for most of the evening. She stayed out of Tracy's way, helped Joan bathe

Corinne, and then sat quietly in front of the television, watching her heartthrob get out of a jam on "C.H.i.P.S." Eventually, though, after the fire had been put out, and Tracy had emerged from hiding and apologized, and we were finally able to gather peaceably in the livingroom and eat the cake that Lois and I had baked for one last farewell fling, a gleam of fear flashed in Katie's placid eyes.

She sat on the floor at Bernie's feet, her head pressed against his leg. Her untouched piece of cake lay on the floor beside her, and her fingers played with the icing. "If I can't do my homework at the new school, can I send it to you so you can help me wiff it?" she asked in a small, frightened voice.

Bernie pulled her head up so he could look her in the eye. "I think you'll do just fine," he said. "But if you have problems, I'm sure that your teachers will help. Or your new parents."

"Will wou come wisit me?"

Jason toughened his voice. "Come on, babe," he said. "Sit up tall. It's all going to be fine. You're only going to Las Cordilleras, you know. Not Timbuktu."

"Timbuktu," James echoed, laughing.

"Timbuktu, fuck you," said Tracy, under her breath.

Katie laughed with the rest of us as Richard reached over to give Tracy a gentle swat on the leg, but her cake remained uneaten. "You want my piece, Trace?" she asked at last.

I watched Tracy struggle, wondering whether her love of cake would break through her determination to ignore the entire event. It did. "Thanks," she said. She grabbed the plate and stuffed huge forkfuls into her mouth, swallowing the bites without tasting them. She ran her finger over the plate to collect the crumbs, then licked them off with a loud sucking sound and put the plate back next to Katie on the floor. Then burped, loudly.

At last we got them all to bed, all asleep. Finally relaxed, we sat in the kitchen gossiping and writing in the daily log. And then we heard the screams.

I have heard people scream before, of course. I have screamed myself. I have heard screams of people on roller coasters, or in horror movies, or wild games of tag. I have heard screams that began in the throat, and soared with excitement and exhilaration through the vocal chords and out of the mouth. They are light screams, as weightless as a whistle. But these were different. These were heavy screams, screams of terror. They began deep inside, in the stomach, and heaved themselves out, carrying with them the rough, tortured material of the soul. They were violent screams, uncontrolled, alive, and they brought with them their own history, their own pain. My hands grabbed my ears, trying to block the noise, but they seeped in through my nose, my eyes, my mouth. Their touch made my bones stiffen, and my stomach grew cold.

"Katie," said Lois, but Jason was already halfway down the hall to her. We arrived a second behind him, and found her not in a puddle of blood but in bed, asleep, and screaming with all her might, "No! No!"

"Katie, wake up, babe. Katie, it's okay. I'm here. It's Jason, honey. You're okay," and Katie, half awake, threw her arms around his neck and sobbed, "No, no, please don't let him get me, please don't let him. Oh, God, no . . ."

Jason shooed us out of the room and sat with her until the terror went away, until she knew where she was, at the RTC with people who loved her, not home with a father who was coming to her bed yet again, for that was what the nightmare had been. For an hour Jason rocked her back and forth, back and forth, soothing her slowly back to sleep. When he came out, she was asleep and his eyes were filled with tears.

The next morning, though, she seemed to have recovered. Even the baby talk was gone. She held her head high, shoulders back as she packed her things into a duffle bag and small suitcase that we had given her as a going-away present. She lined us all up in a row and moved down it like a bride down a receiving line, saying good-bye to each one of us. When she got to Jason, she reached into her bag and handed him the ashtray. "You keep it," she said. "I made it for you, really." And if there was a tiny bit of desperation in the huge final hugs she gave us before she got into the shiny brown station wagon and slammed the door, she got in all by herself, with a smile and a wave, and hardly a backward glance.

Franklin

The graveyard lay at the end of the town like a dog curled languid and panting on a stoop. The air there felt thick and warm and moist, filled with souls who wrapped themselves around you, like the clouds of swarming gnats, and pressed you into the earth. The sun was hotter there than in town; it grew stronger past the gas station, past the post office and grocery store, past the bar, the motel, the two flower shops, past the houses spaced farther and farther apart, its rays like burning cattle prods, urging you on. There was a sign as you got to the edge, whose worn and faded letters proclaimed a bargain, a promise: choose your gravestone now, free, with no obligations, just call. Beyond the sign, stretching out for rows and rows, were the memorials already chosen, obligations met, line after line of whitewashed wood and stone, standing out against the green of the meadow and the deep blue of the endless sky, alight and alive with hundreds of brilliantly colored flowers, bouquets covering each grave, flashing out spirits from each plot.

Among the homemade whitewashed crosses with the rough, penknifed names and dates hewn down the upright bar were scattered proud and lofty vaults of ivory-colored stone, which lifted the bodies inside up out of the earth, preserving and protecting. Under the crosses, under the ground, even the rotting bodies were resurrected by a photograph of the person who used to be, the women surrounded by their families, the men most often in uniform, scowling proudly, and the few children, smiling and innocent, eyes staring off into the distance, and all, all framed by the vibrant reds, yellows, violets and blues of the flowers.

I liked to go at twilight, when the dying rays of the sun deepened and brought to life the colors of the plain. I went there often by myself. But of all the children, Franklin, eleven years old and unafraid, was the only one willing to come with me.

Not that the others didn't share a fascination with death. But they liked it sterilized, cleaned up—as when they begged me one day to take them to the town mortuary. We went on a whim, and they listened in terrified rapture to the undertaker explain how he drained the blood out of the bodies with tubes like *this* and channeled it into *that* tub, and dressed it with clothes chosen by the family from *this* rack, and placed it into one of *those* coffins (as the kids stood around, arguing about who had "first dibs" on which coffin for themselves) and then smiled at his offer to take us all in the back for a game of pool. But they found the old graveyard boring. Dumb. Spooky. They refused to go.

So Franklin and I would go together, and he would repeat for me stories his grandmother, a Spanish *curendera*, had told him, of Indian magic and spirits and souls—stories that were easy to believe as we lay hidden in the tall grasses on the far side of the graveyard in the gathering twilight. Everything, he told me, had a soul, from the mightiest human to the lowliest lizard ("Lizard," he said to me. "You are my Lizard.") to the tiniest twig, and any time you killed an animal, you must first ask its permission, explain to it why you were forced to murder it, or else its soul would come back and haunt you, making you sick. Unless, he said, you knew how to ward off the evil spirits (eat a jalapeño each morning and night), or had access to a *bruja*, or witch, who could give you cures . . .

"How do you know these things?" I asked.

"My grandmother told me," he answered.

Franklin had come to us because he pulled a knife on a girl on his school bus and later stabbed a male teacher. Also because he arrived at school each day higher than a kite on pot and pills and mushrooms and cacti that most of us had never even heard of, although the school had never seemed to notice or care much about it until the "other incidents."

"Why did you do it?" we asked him, before he was admitted, to make sure his violent streak was not "chronic."

"He told me to suck his dick," Franklin said. "Ain't no one gonna get me to do that."

"And the girl?"

"*Hodito,* man. I was just showing my knife to her and she got all freaked out. That wasn't my fault."

And so we let him in.

I remember him the night he came: the tense, tough, little-boy body held like a boxer's, expecting a quick right to the jaw from any corner at any moment, the watchfulness of his eyes, staring out from under the straight black hair, and the laughter, filling the room. No one, it seemed, had ever teased him before.

"And then," we said, "after you're done hauling all the stones, we sometimes let you have a little bread and water . . . "

He squared his shoulders to take the blow, to show he could take it, until he saw Tracy begin to giggle in the corner. And then the teeth flashed strong and white in his face, his body loosened, doubling over, unable to contain the rush of laughter.

"*Hodito,* man. You guys are crazy!" repeated over and over as Bernie and Richard, buoyed by the new audience, outdid themselves and the other kids for a flash of that smile.

"You're crazy!" as Bernie calmly bit into one jalapeño after another.

"You're crazy!" as Richard juggled three eggs and a grapefruit.

"Hey, that kid's crazy!" as Corinne, high on the energy, began her twisting butterfly dance across the livingroom floor, tearing off her clothes as she went.

He named me Lizard and singled me out, testing me over and over again with his tricks and his temper and his refusal to conform to the rules. One day in early March, just after he came to us, he ran away from me in the parking lot as we left the restaurant where I had taken him for lunch as a special treat because he had been so good all morning. He had not yet learned to handle praise, and I had not yet learned to hold it back. And so, "Good kid," I said, and he was gone, racing down the street with me, far slower, tearing after him, screaming crazily at passersby to stop that child. Half a mile later, he jumped out at me from behind a post where he had hidden when he saw that I couldn't run fast enough to catch him.

"You're slow, Lizard," he said, barely breathing hard. "I could have gotten away if I'd wanted to and been half way back to Tres Angeles before you could have even found anyone to go after me."

"You're probably right," I said, gasping for breath as I held him close.

"And I'm wearing my boots! And you're wearing sneakers!"

"Yes," I said. "You can run faster than I can. But I'm glad you decided not to go. I'd miss you, you know."

He smiled then, and burrowed into my body for a hug.

Unlike the other kids, Franklin seemed capable, almost from the first, of loving another person, and it seemed to me that it would be his salvation. Because, unlike the other children, he had known love. If his mother ignored him, if there was no father, if his brothers gave him drugs and then beat him when he was too high to fight back, there was still his grandmother, who would take him and stroke him and tell him stories about animals and trees and sky, which he would repeat to me in the quiet of our graveyard or up on the roof, where he liked to go to watch the sun set.

It was she, he said, who had taught him how to use a knife, and it was not easy to convince him that stabbing another person was wrong, no matter what. Hard, too, to convince him that he could not carry knives around with him at the center, and harder still to keep him from stealing them from the kitchen and keeping one with him regardless. And hardest of all to punish him when, with just such a stolen knife, he spent an entire rest period hollowing out wood to make pot pipes, one for each of the staff, which he presented to us when he emerged from his room that afternoon, with the announcement that they worked, too, and if we'd only give him some stuff, he could show us just how well.

Franklin came to us in March. In early April, I moved from my quarters in the RTC (a storeroom at the back of the house that only locked from the outside, where I was awakened each morning by the thudding of Paul's feet and his high-pitched screaming as he galloped down the long hall to escape his teacher, who ran after him with the clothing he needed to wear that day) to a cabin up in the mountains, where I awoke to the sound of a horse's hooves kicking against the wall, asking for breakfast.

The cabin was small: one large, rectangular room, with a greenhouse built of what seemed to be giant sheets of plastic wrap nailed to one end. On sunny days, even in the coldest part of winter, the greenhouse was a warm place to sit and read a book. The only heat in the rest of the cabin came from a wood stove in the center of the room, which I would stuff full of logs before I went to sleep at night, falling asleep in the clammy heat only to wake, freezing, just before dawn when the fire burnt low. I would lie in the warmth from my own body inside the sleeping bag, listening to the stream rush by outside the door, and the lapping sound of deer drinking from it, until I could summon the courage to plunge myself into the icy air and stoke the fire so that it would keep me warm enough for another few hours of sleep. In the mornings I would awaken again and sit up in bed, pulling my sleeping bag around my shoulders, looking through the window at the deep blue mountains and the valley below. Twice the pipes froze, and I spent unhappy weeks pulling my clothes on under the covers, and fighting with Tracy over the shampoo at the RTC. But I didn't mind much.

For to me, a city child, the cabin was a long-dreamed-of refuge. I would lie in the sun on top of the tool shed, reading or thinking about why it was, really, that I had needed so badly to escape. I thought about the love I had felt for my boyfriend, my friends, my parents, and how I had allowed it to die by not getting angry when I should have, not asserting myself when I needed to, harboring resentments that would have been diffused in the open air had I only let them out. It is easy, I found, to feel love in the sunshine of the mountains, to feel that love is a physical force, that must be felt with the whole body, making me want to crush my breasts in the wind's embrace, to leap up the mountain, to stretch out my arms and squeeze air rushing by me. I would look up, sometimes, from a book that I was reading, watch my horse and my kitten frolicking in the grass, and think to myself: This is good. I am happy.

Sometimes, more and more often as the year went on, Bernie would come and stay with me. Like me, Bernie was a refugee, born and bred in the smell of the Chester, Pennsylvania, factories, trying to grow as his father slowly died of multiple sclerosis. He had tried more escapes than I had: into drugs and alchohol and the seamy life of the city's street people before finally finding a haven in the mountains, but our shared knowledge of delis and the theater and the pound of the Atlantic ocean drew us to each other. He was a wild child, in many ways as scared and vulnerable and hurt as the children we worked with, and with equally formidable defenses. "I'm as crazy as you are," he would say to the kids as he staged jalapeño-eating contests or raw egg slurps or invented silly stories about two Indian princesses, Hiawatha and Pocahontas. "Hiya, Watha," he'd say, and the kids would answer "How ya, Polka?" and then they would all scream together: "Two left feet!" and roll on the floor, laughing.

There were other sides to Bernie's craziness as well, that weren't so charming. He was a heavy, needy drinker, for one, dependent on those five or six tall ones he would kick back after work. And he was a storyteller, making up his life as he went along, mixing fact with fantasy like different colored paints, until the original hues were lost. But I did not understand these sides of him until much later. When we were together, Bernie would show me only the joyful part of himself. He would bring fresh shrimp or scallops from the market in town, and we would sauté them in my old cast-iron frying pan and then eat them with chopsticks as we stood over the stove and got happily drunk on bad white wine. He would bring his dog, too, his shaggy sheepdog Abraham, to play with my kitten and we would laugh at them, all of us tumbling together on the rough woven rug.

Abraham was the dumbest dog I had ever met. Bernie had rescued him from the pound one day, and, like the Indians in the legend, because Bernie had saved his life, Abraham was his slave forever. Abraham, who would be lying under a table and spring up so quickly when Bernie walked in the door that he would crack himself on the head and walk around in a daze for an hour. Abraham, who would throw himself at the truck as we pulled into the driveway, so happy was he to have his master home again. Abraham, who would come with me when I rode my horse, Darcy, whom I bought in the summer as the fulfillment of a childhood dream, inevitably getting himself tangled in the horse's legs. And Abraham, who would dance around the cabin with Bernie holding his front paws up in the air, swirling and swirling to silly country songs. I think Bernie saw himself in Abe: slightly slower than the rest, out of sync, the class clown who always despised himself because he couldn't measure up, the youngest son, sacrificed to a hostile world by parents who didn't understand and didn't care.

It was fun, being with Bernie in my cozy cabin. He would make me laugh late at night with magic tricks, or tell me stories, real or imagined, about his past as his turbulent gray eyes stared up at the ceiling. If he never understood, or cared, what went on inside of me, well, even that was a good antidote to the all-too-intense relationship that had been so large a part of the reason I'd escaped to the Southwest in the first place. All in all we were a happy family.

But of course, the kids hated it, especially the boys. Especially Franklin.

One Saturday in July, a few weeks after school had let out for the summer and I had begun working with the house kids full time, Bernie and I came into the kitchen together. He was munching on his usual breakfast burrito and swigging out of a Coke bottle, and I was spooning raspberry yoghurt out of a container with a plastic spoon. The morning sun felt hot, and Bernie and I talked about an all-day fishing trip.

Franklin was clearly not in a good mood. "Hey, Bernie, man. What kind of breakfast is that?" he asked, as soon as we walked in the door.

"A Southwest special."

"Well, give me a bite."

"Sorry," said Bernie, shaking his head. "If I give you a

bite, I've got to give everyone a bite, and then there'll be nothing left for me."

"So? You're too fat already."

I smiled at Franklin's pre-adolescent pudginess. "You're none too skinny yourself, kiddo," I said.

"Oh yeah?" he said, glaring at me. "Well, who asked you?" There was real anger in his voice, way out of proportion to my tease, or so I thought.

"Hey, calm down," I said. "I was only kidding."

"*Puta,*" he said, in a voice that was soft but clearly intended to be audible.

Philip looked up from his comic book. "Hey, that's ten push-ups," he said.

"Yup, that's right," said Bernie. "Ten for Frankie, for cursing, and ten for you, for butting in."

I laughed.

"What's so funny? Whore." Franklin said.

"Franklin—"

"Whore!" he screamed, running from the room with me, Bernie, and the other kids close behind. Bernie got to him first, cornered him in the living room where he stayed, crouched and ready to fight.

"Okay," Bernie said to him. "You need to come back to the kitchen now and do some calming down. Okay?"

"Fuck you," Franklin said.

"Get the other kids into the kitchen," Bernie said to me. I turned to go.

"Yo!" Philip screamed. "He's got a knife!" I whirled around to see a flash of metal and Bernie, in control, grabbing Franklin's wrist and twisting it behind his back, shoving him belly first onto the floor. He pried open the boy's fingers and took the knife.

"*Chingasa!*" Franklin screamed, but it was to me that his

anger was directed. "*Puta!* Whore!" even as Bernie held him down.

"Maybe you should watch him," Bernie said. "Do you think you can?"

Not at all sure, I said, "Sure," and took over Bernie's position, holding the boy's brown wrist hard, halfway up his back, my weight resting on the small of his back, my ankles locked over his to keep him from kicking me.

This transfer of power only made Franklin angrier. "So, you like to fuck Bernie, huh?" he said. "Do you like his dick in you?" I stiffened but kept silent, flushing defensively even as I told myself not to take it personally, not to respond, not to get angry myself. Just let him get it out. And he did, spewing hate and hurt and rage up at me, as I sat on his back and thought about how I had sat with him a few nights before in the graveyard, sharing his grandmother's magic. Thinking, I love you, kid. I love you. "Who else do you like to fuck?" he was asking. "Do you like little kids? Is that why you work here? Huh? Or is it just because you can't get anyone your own age?"

He screamed on and on, and I thought about anger, how much I had always feared it, and the lengths to which I had gone, sometimes, to avoid its being directed at me. That was one of the things that had gone wrong at school, I realized: there had been so many people telling me what to do, contradictory things, and to avoid their anger, I had tried to do all of them, losing myself in the process. Yet here I was, sitting on the back of this boy I loved, holding his wrist almost to his shoulder blades as he cursed at me, hating me. And I was not wounded. I saw, suddenly, the beauty of a place like the RTC, a place where losing control was safe, where you could scream and curse and let out the rage and frustration of a lifetime, and someone would always be there to stop you before you went too far. I tightened the pressure on his wrist, thinking, okay, kid, get it out, let it all out, and when it is all over, we will still love each other just as much. Maybe even more.

Finally, after what seemed like hours of this, his body relaxed, and he was quiet. "Let me go," he said.

"Not until you show me you can control yourself."

"I'm calm. I can control myself. Let me up."

"Okay," I said, "but we need to do some talking."

He began to cry, softly. "Okay . . . but please let me go."

I released my grip on his arm and stood up, but he remained on the floor, his tears dropping silently onto the rug.

"I'm sorry, Lizard," he said.

"I know. It's all right."

"You hate me now."

"No, Frank . . . I don't hate you. People get angry sometimes, and say things they don't mean. It's all right."

He sat up and looked at me for the first time. "I didn't really mean what I said."

"I know."

Looking down again, he picked at the rug and was quiet for a few minutes. Finally, he said, "Do you love Bernie?"

"Well . . . " I began. And then, for the first time, I heard the question behind the question. I knew that he did not really care whether I loved Bernie or not. He cared only whether I loved him. Franklin. That was what he really wanted to know, what the whole scene, I thought suddenly, had been about. So I said, "Well, I care about Bernie, of course. But I care about you, too. I love you."

"I love you, too, Lizard," he said and plowed his way into my arms.

After a few seconds, he disentangled himself. "Does this

mean I get to go to the movies tonight?" he asked, a small gleam in his eye.

I sighed. "No. I'm sorry—"

"But—"

"It has nothing to do with what happened between us. Like I said, people get angry and say things they don't mean. You already said you were sorry, and I believe you, and as far as I'm concerned, that's that. It's okay to get angry. But it's not okay to carry a knife, and it's very, very not okay to pull it on anyone, for any reason. You were told last time that the next time it happened you would be grounded for a week and lose weekend activity privileges, and that's the way it has to be. I'm sorry."

"But Lizard—"

"No buts, kid," I said, faking an authority I didn't really feel. "Now go to your room, and I'll send Bernie in so that you can apologize to him."

Much to my amazement, he went. And I sank down onto the couch and cried.

The next day, Sunday, was my day off. I had planted a garden in back of the house after paying the farm kids to help me turn over the soil, which was now thick and black and tender. I had planted seeds as the catalogues had said, little sprinkles poured gently into three-inch holes, and had watched in amazement as tiny green sprouts poked out through the heavy earth, as though I were responsible for a miracle. The tomatoes filled me with joy: fat and succulent, still green, but with tantalizing streaks of orange beginning to appear around their stems, covering the thick stalks, bowing them with their weight. I was weeding carefully around them, pulling out each blade of nut grass as if it were an enemy spy, when I heard Abraham yelp.

"What is it?" I said, looking over at him. He looked up, panting, but didn't move. I called him again but got only a whimper in response. "Oh, all right," I groaned, pulling myself to my feet.

When I got closer, I saw that he had gotten tangled in the barbed wire that separated the garden from the rest of the meadow. I reached down to pull him free, but his hair was too matted, and the barb too deeply enmeshed. I sighed, and Abe reached back to lick my hand.

"You really are an idiot, you know that?" I said. He licked my hand again, and I started back up to the cabin, to get a knife. Abe decided that I had abandoned him to his fate and began barking furiously. I shouted reassurances at him, but he kept barking and dancing around until I returned with the knife.

"Hold still," I told him, as I sawed away the matted fur. He yelped suddenly, and reached around as if to bite my finger, baring his teeth. Pulling Abe's fur away from the wire as best I could, I cut through the wire on either side of the entanglement. Suddenly free, Abe bounded away from the barbs before they could grab him again and crawled under the house, where he remained for the rest of the day, ignoring my calls.

"Have it your way," I said to him, and, after fixing the fence with duct tape and some extra wire, I went back to my tomatoes.

I was lying in the sun on top of the shed reading when Bernie drove up, done for the day with work and the bars. Abraham, who had refused to come out for me, scrambled up from his hideout and threw himself at Bernie as he walked up the path to the door. As Bernie scratched Abe's head, I told him what had happened. He ran his hand over the dog's leg.

"I don't feel anything," he said. "Abe must have pulled the rest of the wire out himself. Listen, I just came to get you. Michael Murphy is playing at the Motherlode tonight, and Richard and Jason said they'd like to go. You?"

"Michael Murphy, isn't he the one who does 'Wildfire'?"

"Yeah."

"But I hate that song."

"No . . . but he does other stuff, too. You'll like it, I promise. And we can do some two-steppin'."

"If you get drunk enough."

"Don't worry. I will."

"I wasn't worried."

And off we went. Abe seemed fine all week, and the vet was so expensive, Bernie said. Dogs heal themselves, he said, and people would, too, if they weren't always running off to those goddamned Park Avenue doctors, and Abe was his dog anyway, and didn't I trust him to take care of him, and would I please shut up and stop worrying.

About a week later, Bernie's day off, we were all sitting around in the kitchen talking about what we should make for dinner. There was a funny smell in the air. Tracy faked a gag when I tapped Corinne's bottom to see whether she had defecated in her pants, but she was dry.

"Pee-you," Philip said, coming in from his room. "Tracy cooking tonight or something?"

"Very funny," said Tracy. "I think Franklin must have farted, or something."

"I did not," Franklin said. "You did, probably."

"Did not."

"It must just be something in the air," I said.

By evening, we had all gotten used to it, and I was surprised when Jason came in for the evening shift and remarked on it. "You better get Bernie to give that old dog of his a bath," he said, shooing Abe out of the room. I thought it strange, as we had given him a scrubbing just the week before. After dinner, when the kids had gotten settled in front of the television, I sought out Abraham, who was sleeping in the laundry room. Jason was right, he did stink. "Who have you been playing with?" I asked him. "Don't you know better than to go messing with a skunk?" Abe licked my hand, then began nursing his leg, the one which had been caught the week before.

Bending down, I pulled his fur away. I saw a flash of pink, and pulled back his fur to reveal a gaping hole in his leg, maybe two inches in diameter. His flesh felt warm, as though I could feel the blood coursing through the veins, but the fluid looked white. I wondered, and then I saw: the leg was pulsing not with blood but with maggots, the movement of dozens of maggots, little white worms burrowing in and out through the flesh. Sickened, I pulled back. The stench was almost overpowering. God damn it, Bernie, I thought. Why couldn't you have taken your fucking dog to the doctor like I told you to? Why hadn't I insisted?

Cursing us both, I told Abe to stay and went to call Bernie, who was out. Probably getting drunk, I thought. Just great.

"How 'bout a game of backgammon?" asked Philip, thrilled to discover me alone and available for attention.

"I can't right now," I said, "but how'd you like to do me a favor?"

His shoulders slumped over and he sighed. "What?"

"Abe is hurt, and I want you to help me keep him quiet while I take care of him."

"What do I have to do?"

I took a small paring knife from the kitchen drawer. "Just hold him still," I said. Philip agreed at first, but wavered in the stench of the laundry room.

"This is making me nauseous," he complained the minute we stepped through the door.

"You can't be it if you can't spell it."

"Huh?"

"Oh, never mind. Look, you don't have to do it if you don't want to. But could you please send someone else down? And Phil, not Tracy, okay?"

Franklin appeared in the doorway a few minutes later. "Philip said you needed me. What's the matter?" He paused, sniffing the air like a cat. "Whew! Did Abe cut one, or what?"

"No, Abe cut himself last week, and I . . . guess it never healed properly. Do you think you can help me patch him up?"

"What do you want me to do?"

"Just hold his head and try to keep him still while I try to clean out the cut a little."

He sat with me for hours in the tiny, stinking laundry room, stroking Abraham's head and murmuring snatches of Spanish lullabies while I dug maggots out of the furry, festering flesh. My eyes were riveted on the white worms tunnelling in and out through the exposed pink mush. Not knowing what else to do, I took the tip of the knife and tried to dig them out, one at a time. Abe winced, and once reached around as if to bite me, but he only stared with soft brown eyes and licked my hand. Franklin was crying, his tears falling onto Abe's matted fur as he stroked the dog's head and crooned tuneless words into his ear.

But the more worms I dug out, the more there seemed to

be. The pile of mashed white streaks on the slate floor beside me was making me sick.

"He's gonna die, huh?" Franklin asked me, his eyes full of tears.

"No," I said. "I don't think so."

Franklin nodded. "He is. I've seen this before. He is."

We were getting nowhere. I told Franklin to wait while I went to get a bottle of hydrogen peroxide that we kept locked in the medicine cabinet, along with James's Lithium, Mike's Ritalin and assorted Band-Aids and cold syrups.

"Hold tight now," I said, returning. "This is going to hurt." I poured the clear liquid onto a clean rag and pressed it onto the cut. Abe's breathing grew labored, and Franklin's grip tightened on his fur, but neither of them moved. "Okay," I said. "That's probably all we can do, for now." Together, we told Abe what a good dog he had been, and that everything was going to be all right.

"You did a really terrific job," I told Franklin. "I'm proud of you." Exhausted, I picked up the bottle of disinfectant and turned to follow Abe into the TV room.

"Hey, Lizard," Franklin said. "Here, you forgot this." He picked up the knife and handed it to me. He smiled suddenly. "See, I'm not so bad, am I?" he said.

"Nope," I said, smiling back at him. "Not so bad at all."

Abe didn't die, of course. After hearing my hysterical lectures, my opinion that he wasn't fit to have a dog in the first place, Bernie finally agreed to take him to the vet, a kind looking man with sharp blue eyes, who told me that I had done a good job, poured another batch of disinfectant into the wound, and then put in a couple of stitches and told us to come back when and if the infection did.

Abe held none of his pain against either of us, which is more than could be said for me. Franklin went around for the next two weeks with his chest puffed out and his shoulders thrown back. Each time we were alone he would ask me whether I remembered how we fixed Abraham together. Each morning he would run to the dog and check him over to make sure the wound was healing properly, running back to fill me in on the nuances of his progress.

From then on, slowly, Franklin began to feel that maybe he really was not so bad, after all. And if he was not so bad, then perhaps he did not need to act so bad, to be punished quite as much. Slowly, he opened up, grew calmer, slower to anger. He made friends with James and the two of them would go exploring together, or hunting for arrowheads, the small, quick boy leading the way as the tall, pale one followed behind, bending down to catch what Franklin was saying.

School resumed in September. Having decided, shortly after the Abe incident, that he wanted to be a veterinarian, Franklin now announced that he needed to learn how to read, a skill that he had until that point stubbornly maintained that he possessed, despite our knowledge to the contrary. He was not easy to teach. For each letter he learned he forgot two more, and the fury of his frustration often meant the destruction of the books and flashcards I worked for hours to construct. One dreary November afternoon he confided in me that he was retarded and that was why he could not learn. I asked him what had given him that idea, and he looked surprised and said that his mother had told him, lots of times.

"Come on," I said, "I'm going to prove to you that you're

wrong." I took out a piece of paper and wrote on it all the words that he had learned over the past three months: man, can, ran, fan, pan, ban, mat, sat, cat, fat, flat, drat, hat, and on and on, twenty-five of them, filling up practically the whole page. "Here," I said. "You read this to me. And then we'll see who's retarded." He jumped up then, and spilled some juice and had to go and clean it up and then he had a stomachache and then he was tired and he'd do it tomorrow, but finally he sat down and began to read, one word at a time, slowly at first then faster and faster as he saw that he could do it, and when he was done he looked up in amazement and said, "Hey, I can read." And then louder, "Hey, man, I can read!" And then a shout, "I can read! Far out! I didn't know I could do that!" Then he grabbed me by the arm and dragged me into the kitchen, shouting "I can read! I can read!" sounding off the words to each new person he could find.

It was wonderful, too, to sit with him in the stillness of the twilight in the graveyard or on the roof and talk of life, both his and mine. For by November it was clear to both him and to the staff that there was no need for him to remain at the center once his year was up in March. The staff thought it would be best to place him with his aunt, a sane, responsible-seeming woman in Las Cordilleras, far from his abusive brothers and indifferent mother. But Franklin steadfastly maintained that he wanted to go home. I was going home soon, too, my year in the Southwest being almost up, and a new semester at Harvard just around the bend of the new year. We talked about it one night, in the graveyard, watching the sun set.

"Where do you want to go when you leave here?" I asked him. "Don't you think you'd be better off in Las Cordilleras?"

"I want to go home," he said. "Everyone wants to go home. Even you, Lizard."

"No, I don't," I said. But then I began to picture my street, and the noises and smells I had grown up with, my family and friends who suddenly seemed very far away. "Well, maybe you're right," I said. "I guess part of me does want to go home. Does get homesick. It's true."

He thought awhile, then looked up at me. "Part of you wants to go home to your family and friends in New York," he said. "But you also have a home here, in the mountains, with the animals and the beautiful land. And part of you wants to be here, too."

I hugged him. There was nothing more to say.

He found a way to tell us the rest of it, without words. To let us know the surging fear that lurked just out of sight, a shadow away from the sweetness of the stories he told, the hunger of his body when he begged to be cuddled. A month before I was to leave, another boy arrived at the RTC, Jack, a tall, hulking kid, out of control and given to violent rages. Hating Frankin on sight, Jack picked him up one day and slammed him against the wall as hard as he could.

Immediately afterward, Franklin seemed fine. He laughed a little, even, as if to show Jack that he couldn't be destroyed that easily. But when I went to call him to dinner, I found him sitting on his bed, sweating, eyes glazed, gripping the wooden handles of his numchucks so that the wire was stretched taut between them, staring straight ahead. Ready to kill. Eleven years old, he frightened me.

"Hey, kiddo," I said, "what's up? Do you want to talk, or do you just need some space?"

Silence. Pale, shallow breathing.

"Do you want to talk, or do you just want to be alone?"

He was not there. Sweating, staring, hate and terror in his eyes.

"Are you sick?"

Silence. Then: he was up, poised, ready to wrap the wire around my throat, to kill me without knowing it was me. I was afraid. But there was enough control left in him, barely, to see the miles between me and his brothers José, Luis, Felipe. "Get out," he growled. He was to be taken seriously, I thought. It was a threat, a command.

I ran out into the hall to Richard, sitting in the kitchen, drinking a cup of tea. "Franklin is going to kill somebody," I said, and Richard laughed, until he saw that I was not kidding. I heard a scream, then Franklin dashed out into the hall, stopped dead on the floor by Richard's flying tackle. Bernie ran to help, but even their combined weight was not enough to still his kicking thrusts. I grabbed his legs and he fought against me, stiffening his muscles, his eyes squeezed shut. He was far away.

"Franklin!" said Richard. "Where are you? Come back. Where are you, kid? Come on, join us, come back." Franklin twisting, sweating, crying, moaning.

Then silence. He seemed dead. His arms were limp, even his breathing seemed to have stopped.

We got off him, opened his shirt, rubbed his chest, his hair, his wrists, called him, loved him, urged him back. No response. Throughout, I was conscious that I was smiling, my mouth frozen upward, too upset and frightened to absorb what was happening.

When he didn't wake up, even Bernie and Richard began to get frightened. Richard looked at me, said maybe we should take him to the hospital, so I got a quilt to wrap him in, but as I laid my cold hands on his chest he was suddenly awake, whimpering in terror, trying to push his way into Richard's skin for comfort. Then he turned, and tried to run.

"Where are you?" Richard asked. "Who is after you?"

Franklin screamed. "José! Louisssss!" He kicked the quilt off and struggled against Richard's arms, but in his eyes I could at last see a still shaky but growing awareness of where he was. Slowly he stopped struggling and was quiet. He rubbed the tears from his eyes, like a drunk waking up from a bender with people who had seen actions that he cannot remember performing.

"Do you know where you are now?" Richard asked.

He jumped out of Richard's arms, looking at him as though he were nuts. "Of course I know where I am. At the RTC. What are you? Crazy?"

He was back.

The Farm Kids

In the mornings, I sat at the long kitchen table. I read the log book to see what had happened during the night and drank camomile tea, comforted by the familiar din. The kitchen was warm and safe: Jason, in his deep bass voice, would greet Tracy, give her a hug and then send her back to change into clean clothes; Franklin and Philip would fight over the comics; Paul would finish his cereal and clutch the empty bowl to his chest, rocking and murmuring ouiouiouiouioui; Corinné would play dreamily with her spittle and crawl into Lois's lap for kisses. And then five days a week, nine months a year, the farm kids would arrive, and Tracy, appearing in a new set of soiled clothes, would shout, "The farm kids are here!" And Bernie and I would have to gulp the last of our breakfast and walk up to the schoolhouse to greet them.

Most of the children at the farm went to public school,

some of them even went on to college. But there were a few, seven to be exact, who were sent to us. There was Mike Jonas, for one. He was a small, slight fourteen-year-old, smart and serious but hyperactive, with an explosive temper. He had bright red hair, flashing blue eyes, and, often, a leering grin. A self-appointed defender of the weak, except when he wanted them to do his bidding, he was the leader of the group. When he was ten, he had watched his mother shoot his father in the head during an argument. He and his older brother, Barry, had been placed at the farm. The next year, Dan Johnson had adopted Barry but not Mike, and the year after that, Mike had begun acting out in school.

There was Alex Running Bear, a full-blooded Cherokee Indian, as he was the first to tell you. He was thirteen years old and had lived in at least fifteen different foster homes and residential centers. This was his sixteenth, and his goal in each was to make life as hellish as he could for everyone before he was sent to the next. A transient, he saw no point in trying to stay out of trouble, or stay in school. He was broad and stocky, and far stronger than I. I was frightened of him and he knew it, using the knowledge to his advantage. He threatened me often, threw rocks at me so that they would just miss my head, twisted my arm behind my back until it felt like it might break, and then released me at the last second. He loved to be punished. If there were demerits to be given out, he would not rest until he was further in the hole than anyone else. If Bernie or Jason got fed up at last and put him in a timeout corner, he would try so violently to escape that both Bernie and Jason's full attention was occupied, shortchanging the rest of the kids. If he were kept home from an outing, he would make life so miserable for the staff who stayed with him that they secretly vowed to let him go the next time no matter what he did, and let the trip staff deal with his misbehavior. As he often told us, he couldn't have cared less. About anything or anybody. And he didn't want anyone caring about him.

There was Tony, the oldest, the biggest, the dumbest. He tested as borderline retarded and should have been in the public school special ed class. He had begun there, but was so upset by being labeled retarded that he devoted all his energy to beating up the other special ed kids until the school refused to have anything more to do with him. Tony was an ugly boy, large and lumbering, with mucus perpetually streaming from his nose and a thin drop of spittle from his mouth. Jason had told me that he was terrified of women, including me, terrified of the feelings they aroused in his sixteen-year-old body. On most days he dealt with his fear by ignoring me completely, but when I broke into his reserve, by asking him to do his work or leave Peter alone, he would quickly lose control. He was devoted to Mike, the only person who ever tried to stick up for him in his various battles, and Tony lived to do his bidding.

There was Steven, a severely handicapped boy, totally deaf, with cerebral palsy which prevented his effective use of the manual alphabet, leaving him virtually no way to communicate his immense anger and frustration except by acting it out. This he did frequently, in violent temper tantrums and battles with children and staff. He came to us in the middle of the year, and we had no resources to enable us to help him. Bernie, Jason and I pleaded with Dan Johnson to send Stevie to a residential school for the deaf in Las Cordilleras, but Dan would not hear of sending one of his charges so far away. So Steven remained with us for two months, occupying at least one staff person's full attention, and constantly distracting the other kids.

Paul and Corinne's brother Peter came from the farm as

well. He lived there now only because his two years at the RTC had done nothing to help him. He still lived in his own locked room, in which every ounce of energy he possessed was spent on refusing to remember all the things he could never forget.

As of March, there were also Jesse and Joe. They were brothers, Mutt and Jeff, eleven and fourteen, who had been arrested in California on charges of armed robbery—they had attempted to hold up a grocery store with a toy pistol—and had spent six months in juvenile detention, a fact of which they were both inordinately proud. How they got to us, no one seemed to know. But from the first they, like the others, were determined to prove to their teachers that they were too cool and too tough to listen to a word that any of us had to say.

On most days, the 100-yard walk to the school house seemed very long.

Alex

Alex was angry at Lois because she had caught him smoking and had taken away not only the cigarette he had in his mouth at the time but his entire pack. Like nearly all of the kids, Alex had a fierce sense of justice. He would have understood if she had just taken the cigarette she'd caught him with, but to take his whole pack, that he had paid for with his own money, was not fair. Forget the fact that smoking was against the rules; those cigarettes were his own personal property, and she had no right to take them. But she did. He sulked through the morning, slumped in his seat, oblivious to everything around him, and at lunchtime he went outside after finishing his hot dogs, picked up a stone, and threw it as hard as he could through the front side window of Lois's blue Oldsmobile station wagon.

Lois came into the classroom that afternoon, interrupting a math lesson.

"I was about to get into my car to drive to a meeting with Dan," she said in her fluttery voice, "when I noticed that the window was broken. I am pretty sure it wasn't broken when I got out of the car this morning." The kids giggled. "Can anyone tell me how it got broken?"

Alex leaned back in his chair, his entire weight resting on the back two legs, balancing dangerously. "Sure. I broke it." He stared into her eyes, his heavy body perfectly balanced in the swaying chair, twisting a rubber band around and around in his fingers. He was daring her to get angry, daring her to punish him, daring her most of all to tell him that he now was not welcome here, in his sixteenth foster home in thirteen years, either.

Lois waited a beat, until all eyes were upon her. Then she said, "Oh." And then, "Alex, dear, don't lean back in your chair like that. You could fall and hurt yourself." Stunned, Alex brought his chair down level with a dull thump.

"I broke it," he said again. "On purpose."

"Do you want to tell me why?"

Alex smiled. Now he was getting some reaction. This was more like it. "Because I wanted to. You took my cigs, I broke your window. You hate me and I hate you. We're even."

"Well, not quite," Lois said. "I don't hate you. In fact, I've always kind of liked you."

"Bull," Alex said, scowling.

Lois smiled. "I do like you, 'Lex, you know. But that still

doesn't make us even. Car windows are a lot more expensive than cigarettes, and a lot better for your health."

"You smoke."

"I know. It's a filthy habit and I wish I didn't."

"I don't smoke. I don't smoke, Lois. Would, would it be good if everyone didn't smoke?" Peter demanded.

"Yes," Lois said. "It would." Alex glared at Peter, pulling the rubber band back and aiming it at his face. Lois caught his attention before he could throw it. "Alex?"

"Yeah?"

"As I said, we're not quite even. I'm still out one car window, and it's supposed to snow tomorrow. I want you to go with Bernie after school and get a new window. You can pay for part of it with your allowance and work the rest off by helping us paint the school this Saturday."

"No way, man! We're supposed to go skiing this Saturday."

"I'm sorry. But there'll be other ski days." Alex muttered something under his breath, but Lois decided not to press him. She turned to go and was almost out the door when Alex stopped her.

"So, Lo . . . uh, after I go get the window with Bernie, then where am I supposed to go?"

"What do you mean?"

"I mean, are you sending me to Las Cordilleras? St. Francis? The RTC? Where?" Lois still looked confused. Alex decided she was torturing him, dragging out the suspense. His voice rose. "Don't I even have a right to know where you're going to put me?" His leg began to jiggle rapidly under the table.

"After you get the window, Bernie will take you home. To the farm. That is where you live. That is where you will live until you are eighteen years old. I thought you understood that."

Alex looked close to tears. "Fine. Don't tell me. I don't care. I don't give a fuck because I hate you anyway."

Lois went to him and began to rub his back, her hand moving in gentle circles over his tense muscles. "You can hate me all you want to," she said, "but we'll still love you and care about you. The farm is your home, no matter what, and that is where Bernie will take you after you get the window." She rubbed her hand through his hair. "And I'll see you tomorrow. Here at school."

Alex looked at her, searching her face for a sign of a smile or wink or some other indication that she was teasing him, but he couldn't find one. Finally, his body relaxed. "Okay," he said, tilting back in his chair again. There was a gleam in his eye. "But if you think I'm sorry about your window, I'm not."

"Okay," she said, shrugging slightly. She started toward the door, but turned to him again, one hand on the doorknob. "And, Alex . . . please don't lean back in your chair like that, dear. You could fall and hurt yourself. And then I would be sorry."

Alex smiled, and brought his chair level with a bang.

Peter

"What if you had all the cars in the world? Would that be good? Would it?" He pressed his face in close, shouting at my nose, light, bright blue eyes staring past my shoulder at the moving road outside the window.

"I don't know, Petey-boy. You tell me."

"What kind of car would you like? How about a van? Would it be good if you had a van? Would it? How about if everyone had a van? If we had all the vans in the world, would that be good? Would it?"

His breath stank. I turned my head slightly. "Would it be good if Peter didn't ask any more questions for five minutes? Would it? Do you think Peter could do that?"

Peter laughed but didn't move his face. A car passed us on the left, speeding, and the eyes widened slightly. "Hey, that car is going at ninety miles an hour! What if the car had no doors? Would that be good? Could the car still drive if it had no doors? Would that be good? What about if the doors were broken? Could the car still drive? What if all the doors in the world were broken? Would that be good? Would it? Would it be good?"

The road sign read LAS CORDILLERAS 45 MILES. Don't speed, I told my foot. You don't want to end up in the papers tomorrow morning. Don't speed.

"Hey, Pete," I said. "How about some ice cream? Would you like that?"

Peter laughed and nodded faintly, not sure if I really meant it.

"Okay. Well, if you can go five minutes without asking any more questions, then you can have an ice cream. Okay? Think you can do that, Pete?"

Silence. Then, "O-okay. Okay. I won't ask any more questions for five minutes. Okay? Will that be—"

"Peter. So, how do you like school these days?"

"I like school. These days."

"What do you like best in school?"

Peter began bouncing on the seat. "I like drawing best. I

like to draw pictures of cars. Would it be good if everyone drew pictures of cars? Would it?"

"Peter. Remember the ice cream. C'mon. No more questions. Okay?"

This time it didn't even slow him down. His eyes glazed, fixed on the telephone posts flashing by outside with perfect regularity. It was hot in the van. Peter's hair was getting dark with sweat, and his voice rose in pitch. "Would, would, would it be good if we got into a car crash? Would that be good? Would it be good if all the cars in the world got into a car crash?"

"What do you think, Peter?" I asked, mirroring, just like I was supposed to. "Do you think that would be good?"

He looked at me, testing, his eyes wondering if I were serious. And laughed nervously. "No, no that wouldn't be good," hoping it was the right answer, watching my face, breathing hard.

"No, I don't think that would be good, either." His body relaxed a bit, and he sighed. Las Cordilleras: thirty-five miles. Getting there. "How about sports, Peter?" I asked. "Do you like sports?" Silence. "How about basketball? Do you like basketball?"

Peter sighed again, hard. "N-no, no. I don't like basketball." He laughed. "Do you? Do you like basketball? Would it be good if everyone in the world liked basketball? Would that be good?"

Maybe if I don't answer the questions it'll work, I thought, and was silent. The questions got louder, shriller, more insistent.

"Would it be good if all the basketballs in the world were broken? What about if all the basketballs in the world were at your house? Would that be good?"

I wanted to tell him to shut up, to push him down on the seat and make him stay there.

"Peter! Could you please sit back?" I asked. There was no response. His breath rushing up my nose was giving me a headache.

"Would it be good if basketballs were as big as houses? Could you still play basketball if all the basketballs were as big as houses? What if they were as big as elephants?" He laughed. "Would that be good? Would it be good if all the cars in the world turned into basketballs? Would it be good? Would you still be able to drive your car if it was a basketball?" More laughter, louder, his face blocking my view of the road. "Would you have to roll down the road in your basketball? Should I draw a picture of a car shaped like a basketball? Would it be good? Would it be good if—"

Las Cordilleras thirty miles. His head was blocking my view of the road, his body rigid and, Jesus Christ, now I was the one going crazy. Compassion, I thought. I thought about what I had heard about how he and Paul and Corinne had lived as children, thought of him hearing his brother's screams from inside a locked closet, of his being forced

"none of the basketballs had doors?"

to change the shoebox that his brother Paul

"Would you still be able to get into them if they had no doors?"

crapped in

"Would it be good? Would it?"

in the closet.

"And what about if the doors were broken? Could you still drive the basketballs if the doors were all broken?"

And thought, Yes Peter, yes honey,

"Would it be good if all the doors in the world were broken? Would that be good?"

if that filled my brain in the silence

"Would it?"

I would ask questions, too. I reached over and mussed his hair, loving, comforting. He shoved his face closer to mine, yelling, louder and louder.

"Could you still drive the cars if all the doors in the world were broken? Could you? What kind of car would you like if you could have any kind of car in the world? Would you like a Corvette? How about if I bought you all the Corvettes in the world? Would that be good? Would it?"

Las Cordilleras twenty-five miles. Still over half an hour. My head was pounding. The road was barely visible over the top of Peter's hair. I couldn't breathe; he smelled; he was pressing in closer and closer.

"Sit down!" I yelled, but he didn't move. His eyes were staring past my ear, fastened on the road outside.

I couldn't breathe.

"Would it?"

I was going to throw up, hit him, shut him up. We were going to crash.

"Would it be good?"

I looked at him. "Hey Peter." He leaned away from me slightly.

"Would it?"

"Peter. Tell me about Paul."

Bright blue eyes staring into mine for just a second.

"Tell me about Paul."

He turned and curled in the corner, huddled against the locked door of the car. He lifted his eyes just above the level of the glass and watched in silence as the telephone poles flashed by with perfect regularity, all the way to Las Cordilleras.

Mike

It was horseback riding day, and Mike was completely out of control.

"Hey, Liz. You know what horseshit smells like?"

I ignored him.

"Do you?" He farted, complete with noise and smell, as the other kids giggled. "That's what!" he shouted triumphantly.

"Funny," I said. "But if you ever want to *see* another horse, let alone smell its shit, you'd better finish up that page of math problems right quick." The kids laughed again, and Mike looked angry. He did not like being upstaged.

"Hey, Bernie," he said. "You let her go around using words like that?"

"I don't speak for the lady. Now finish your fucking math." Mike laughed this time, the tension dispelled.

Math finished, we boarded the van to the farm. "Does, does, does this van have wheels?" Peter asked. Mike was sitting next to him.

"Don't ask dumbass questions if you're going to sit next to me," he said.

"Would it be good if the van didn't have any wheels?"

"I said, shut up."

"Would it be good if all the vans in the world didn't have any wheels?"

Mike punched Peter in the arm. "He, he, he hit me."

I stood up. "That's it. Peter, no more questions. Mike, no more hitting." I was always surprised at the determination with which the kids tried to get themselves in trouble on special days, as though they needed to be denied the treat so that their view of the world as a hateful, hurtful, yet known and therefore safe place would not be threatened.

"Peter, no more questions. Mike, no more hitting," Mike mimicked. His voice was high and squeaky.

I glared at him. Enough was enough. "Anyone who doesn't want to go can get off the van right now." Mike flushed and was quiet. He spent the rest of the ride trying to spit on Alex's arm. Each time he tried, Alex would whirl around and hit him. It didn't look like much fun to me, but they seemed to be enjoying themselves, so I left them alone.

"Hey, there's a Corvette!" Joe yelled, his voice rising with excitement.

"I dubs it," Alex said quickly.

"Uh-uh," Joe said. "I saw it first, so I dubs it."

"Seeing it first don't mean shit. I dubbed it first. It's mine."

Joe looked ready to fight it out then and there. I laughed. "I can't believe you guys are fighting about a car that neither of you can really have."

They both turned on me, suddenly united against a common enemy.

"Could too," Joe said.

"Yeah," said Alex.

"Oh, yeah? How?"

"Steal it!" they shouted together, and laughed. I laughed, too, and we rode the rest of the way in relative peace.

It remained calm until we were saddling up the horses when, for no apparent reason, Joe hauled off and punched one of his horses as hard as he could in the chest. The horse whinnied in pain and surprise, and I felt a cold flash of anger run through me, even as I told myself that he had needed to do it, probably because he was scared of riding and knew no other way to get out of it without losing face. I would help him out.

"Okay, that's it," I said. "No riding for you."

"Good. I don't want to ride these wussy horses anyway."

I know you don't, I thought. I just wish you could find some other way of letting us know. We decided that Bernie would stay behind with him and Peter, who had suddenly decided that he didn't want to go either, while I took Mike, Alex, and Tony for a ride. Or while they take me for one, I thought.

Mike declared himself trailmaster, and I said he was welcome to lead the way as long as we went slowly, because I hadn't been riding in a long time and I needed a little while to get used to it. He agreed, and we started up the trail at a slow trot. It was pleasant, trotting along in the woods on a perfect April day. The mountains around us were still covered with snow, but the sun felt warm and I let it press me downward into the warmth of the horse I rode. I listened to the birds chirp in the trees all around us. I saw an owl see us, turning its head to keep us in the field of vision of its round eyes. Little by little I relaxed into the horse's rocking gait. I closed my eyes and turned my face to the sun, flirting with it, slipping far away into a memory of a sunny spring day at the beach long ago, my boyfriend at my side as we rolled together in the sand. I missed him, suddenly, and thought it might be nice if he were there, if only his being there would not automatically make the scene itself impossible. I opened my eyes again and thought how nice it was for us all to be equal for once, all the same size on the horses. I enjoyed being the follower, watching Mike and the others up ahead frolicking in their rare freedom.

"Can we canter a little?" Mike asked when we got to a straightaway.

I thought for a minute. I did feel awfully comfortable on the horse—I had once been a good rider. And, like the boys, I loved to go fast. "Okay," I said. "But just a canter, Mike. Not too fast." But before I could finish my sentence, Mike's horse sped off down the road at a gallop, with Alex and Tony close at his heels. My horse decided he'd better catch up, and I found myself flying along, my nose pressed against the horse's neck, smelling its sweat. Low branches from the trees stung my face and tore my hair. I clutched with my knees as hard as I could, and cursed English style saddles, which don't even have a pommel to grab, as I flailed about to get a better grip on the reins. I screamed into the wind for Mike to slow down, but he didn't hear me or didn't care. His horse made a sharp turn to the right and mine followed, without me. I landed on the ground with a hard thump as my horse shot down the road.

I was surprised but not hurt. I stood up and brushed myself off, wondering what to do next, and how I was ever going to explain this latest disaster to Bernie, who was patiently waiting with Joe and Peter back at the barn. Meanwhile back at the farm . . . I thought. I wondered how we were ever going to capture my horse.

As soon as he saw my horse, minus me, breeze in front of him, Mike turned and doubled back to me, yelling ahead to the others to wait up.

"You okay?"

I was too embarrassed to be angry. "I think so."

"What happened?"

"Well, someone started going a little fast. Then, I don't know. I guess I zigged when I should have zagged."

Mike laughed. "Don't worry," he said. "Why don't you climb on with me, and we'll go get your horse." Mike helped me up into the saddle and then climbed on in front of me, crouched up practically on the horse's neck. I put my arms around his waist. "Hold on tight, now," he said. The horse sped off beneath us, and I clung to the small body in front of me. As the horse swerved to avoid the trees pressing in on us from all sides, I felt him shift his weight to balance both of us, now egging on, now holding back, totally in control of himself and the animal. Every few minutes he would look back at me to make sure I was all right and tell me I was doing fine, enjoying his role as a protector. We pushed on in the forest, in hot pursuit, and I realized suddenly how relaxed I was on the horse with him, how safe I felt with him leading the way.

"You're a good rider," I said, and felt him smile.

Tony

We had made it through the morning; it was lunchtime. Tony, for once, had finished the dishes without the usual complaints about stomachaches and other ills and begged to be allowed to take a walk with Cindy and me. She was a pretty fourteen-year-old, with us for a few weeks because she had run away from home and refused to go back, and her grandmother, who had agreed to take her, had been hospitalized unexpectedly.

Jason looked dubious. "Why don't you stay here with me and shoot some baskets?"

"I feel like going for a walk."

"Well, why don't you and I take a walk then? Maybe Cindy and Liz have things they want to talk about."

Tony scowled at Cindy. "Do you?"

"No," Cindy said, looking at the ground. "Not really."

"See? So, can I go?"

Jason raised his eyebrows at me, questioning whether I thought I could handle it. I had just been made a full staff member three weeks earlier, on the first of May, and was determined to earn my keep and the respect of the rest of the staff. How bad could it be, anyway? I shrugged and nodded.

Jason still looked reluctant, but gave Tony the okay, and the three of us started off. We walked side by side, me in the middle, Cindy close by my side, Tony a little way off, trying to think of something to say to her.

"See the cows, Cin?" he said at last.

Cindy flashed me a look of disgust, and then looked down. "Uh-huh."

"I can milk a cow."

"Good for you."

"Can you?"

"Uh, no. Actually, I never tried."

"Do you want to? You could come visit me up at the farm, and I could teach you how."

"Uh, no thanks."

We walked to the end of the road together, our silence broken only once, when Cindy asked me, sotto voce, whether I thought Joe was cute. I put my finger to my lips, nodding in Tony's direction, hoping that he hadn't heard. Tony lagged behind a little on the way back. When I turned my head to ask him if he was all right, I saw that he had stopped walking.

"C'mon, Tony," I said. "We gotta get back now. Lunchtime is almost over." He ignored me, staring transfixed at the cows. His mouth was moving rapidly, but no sound was coming out.

"Tony, come *on*," I said, but he gave no sign of having heard. He sniffed loudly, then wiped his nose on the sleeve of his dirty green jacket. As I stood there, wondering what to do, he picked up a handful of stones, and began throwing them at the cows. I moved toward him, but then saw that the cows were safely out of reach.

I didn't know what to do. I knew that anything I did that could be construed by Tony as even vaguely threatening could cause him to lose control altogether. On the other hand, I had to get him back to the house. I stood where I was, and called to him again. "C'mon Tony. Let's go. Now." He whirled around and threw the last stone at Cindy as hard as he could. Then he turned and bolted off across the field. The stone hit her on the leg and she started to cry, but I couldn't stop to help. Instead, I told her to go get help from the house, and took off after Tony, shouting after him to wait, stop, calm down, come back. He ran fast, and I fell farther and farther behind, until he was finally trapped by the barbed wire and thick, ankle-deep May mud at the other end of the field. I closed in on him, stopping about four feet away.

He picked up a rock. "Don't come any closer or I'll kill you. I swear I will."

I had every reason to believe him. "Okay. Come on. No one wants to chase you. No one is mad at you. We understand. Just come on back, and let's talk about it." I was frightened, but Tony was too preoccupied to notice. I could see that he was literally paralyzed, his anger over, wanting to give in, come back, be comforted and forgiven, but unable to let himself. I watched him struggle with himself as he stood there shivering and alone, framed against the mountains, his body splattered with mud.

"C'mon." He took a step toward me, and then saw Jason and Bernie running toward us, with Mike, Alex and Joe trailing in their wake.

"You tell them to stop!" he yelled at me, waving the stone over his head. "Tell them to stop or I'll run, I swear it. I'll run and you'll never catch me."

I looked at him then, his pimpled face contorted with fear and rage, the dull eyes open wide. He was sixteen years old, an age when most boys are begging for the family car to take first dates out to dinner and the movies. And here he was, pathetically lusting after a pert fourteen-year-old who obviously felt he was beneath her, standing in the cold air with snot dribbling down his chin. I wondered how much he hated himself, how much of his difference he understood. He was struggling to maintain the little dignity that we allowed him. At the very least, I thought, he deserves the chance to come back to the house on his own. I hollered at Jason to stop, not at all sure that he would trust me enough to comply, but he did, and the others stopped behind him. Tony relaxed a little. "Now you go, too," he said. "You all go back to the house and then I'll come in."

He still held the rock in his hand, and his eyes looked glazed. I wondered whether he would throw the rock at me as soon as my back was turned, or if he would run away if we left him alone. Part of me thought I must be crazy to trust him again. But more, I hoped that my trust alone might enable him to marshal enough self-control to deserve it. I wondered whether anyone had ever trusted him, and whether it might be too frightening. But he was sixteen years old. It was his choice. If he ran, we could catch him, but if we did not even let him make this choice, I felt, he would be lost forever. I took a deep breath, trying not to let him see how frightened I was.

"Okay," I said. "We'll all go back to the house, and you come in when you're ready." I paused. "I trust you, Tony," I said, but he gave no sign of having heard me. I turned and walked toward Bernie, half expecting to feel the sharp pain of a stone banging against my ear, but there was nothing. I told Bernie and Jason what I had done. Mike, desperate to be the hero, begged to go after him, assuring us that Tony would listen to him.

"I'm sure he would," Jason said. "But this is something Tony needs to do alone." He looked at me and smiled, and suddenly I felt that I had handled the situation right, for once.

We went inside the house without looking back and watched from the window as Tony walked around in small circles, throwing rock after rock into the ground with all his might.

"Let me go to him," said Mike.

"No," Jason said.

Twice he went up to the fence and stared at it, patting it gently, testing it to gauge whether it would bear his weight. Then finally, finally, he straightened and walked slowly back toward the house. Tall and strong and covered with mud, his torn green jacket flapping around him, he walked with a firmer step than I had seen before. Head held high, he marched into the kitchen. He went over to Cindy, who held an ice pack against the bruise on her lower leg where the rock had hit her. For the first time, he looked her directly in the eye.

"I'm sorry," he said. Then he turned and walked slowly back up to the schoolhouse.

Jesse and Joe

The arrival of Jesse and Joe in mid-March ushered in the era of the Great Herpes Scare at the RTC. During their year in California, they had apparently been boy prostitutes and had picked up, as Lois put it, God-knows-what diseases. For the first few weeks all dishes were scrubbed with disinfectant, all lip balm they used was discarded, all sodas they sipped were automatically theirs. Then, people forgot, the rules were relaxed, candy was passed around once again, and they settled into the routine of school.

Jesse, we soon discovered, was a con artist; it was his profession and his passion. He was small and wiry with rough, sandy-blond hair and clear brown eyes shining round and innocent. Jesse would do anything for a dollar: wash your car, wash your dog, clean your house, do your laundry, almost surely sleep with you, although once at the farm that particular source of revenue dried up rather quickly, at least as far as we knew. His raspy voice was unnaturally deep for an eleven-year-old, and he always tried to form words quicker than he could shape them with his mouth, causing him to stutter and making him seem young and vulnerable. From the time I met him, I ached to protect this tough little boy, to give him a sense of security, of love, but I never worried about him. I still don't. I never got to know him very well because he was taken out of school after a few impossible weeks of trying to deal with him and Joe together, and he was given some kind of tutoring up at the farm. I heard he learned to read after only a few months because someone offered him a nickel for every new word he could learn before school let out for the year. I was sorry to see him go; he made teaching impossible when he was there, but it was impossible to teach anyway, and at least he could always make me laugh. He will land on his feet, though, of that I am sure.

Joe was a different story. Joe was mean. He was not openly mean, as Alex and Tony often were; he was sly, devious, sneaky mean. He was mean to those smaller and weaker than he, to Peter and Jesse and Steven, to the house kids, to the animals. He had a slow, mocking smile that spread across his face whenever he did something bad, daring anyone to try to punish him. He lived entirely within the bastion of his self, equally impervious to affection, punishments, warnings, caresses. His life was based on a theory he knew by instinct and experience, that the strong survive while the weak are winnowed out. He liked to catch turtles and light matches under them, to see what they would do. Once he got over his fear of horses, he liked to gallop them until they dripped foam and blood from their mouths. He liked to hold bones out for dogs, calling to them joyously, only to crack the bone over their backs when they came near.

He treated all women with equal contempt. When I asked him how he was doing, he would smile his slow smile and jut his pelvis out in my direction, rubbing his hands over his penis and asking if I really wanted to see how he was doing. He terrorized and titillated Cindy by running his tongue over his blistered lips in a parody of sensuality whenever he got near her and mouthing "I want to fuck you" when he thought our backs were turned. He would come into school in the mornings and drape himself over the low wall that surrounded the schoolhouse, sunning himself. He would push his cowboy hat down over his eyes and tell us all, in a slow, sleepy drawl, how tired he was from all the fucking he had done the night before.

He reminded me sometimes of a young ram, butting his head as hard as he could against everyone he met, showing in every way he could that he was king of the mountain, and never mind the scars he collected in the process. I spent the first two months that he was with us wishing with a pounding head and a throat sore from yelling that he were back in California, giving his treatment to some poor, undeserving soul out there. Until one day, as he went on and on about how much he didn't give a damn, an image flashed into my mind. I saw him suddenly as one of the turtles he tortured, weak and flabby and vulnerable, weighted down by the shell made of lead he carried around with him always, refusing to poke out so much as a head, no matter how hot and uncomfortable it got inside, or how good a little fresh air might feel. And I began to admire him, too, for his refusal to quit, to give up, to die or even to go insane.

I tried to protect his victims from him in every way I could. I made him Abraham's official protector and was gratified to hear him tell the other kids not to play with him too roughly or he would personally break their faces. He began saving Abe scraps from his meat at dinner, bringing them down from the farm in greasy napkins and feeding them to him when he thought no one was looking. I also made him do all the physical work I could: turning over earth for the garden, helping to dig irrigation ditches, stacking sandbags in the spring when there was danger of a flood.

I wish I could say that I cured him, that he was transformed under our loving tutelage from a hooligan into a cherub in the three months we had him at the school, but I can't. On the last day of school, he gave Peter a bloody nose, tried to "cop a squeeze" of Tracy's breast, and screamed curses as he was restrained by Bernie after he refused to go into the timeout space when we asked him to. He was not one to give himself up without a struggle, and chances are good that he will spend much of his life behind bars.

Except on that last day of school, after all his explosions, when he had gone off ostensibly to sulk in the woods, I saw him call Abraham to his side and feed him some greasy cold hamburger and pat his head and smile a little smile when Abe reached up to lick his face.

Philip

I walked into the kitchen one morning in May to find at the table a boy of about fourteen whom I had never seen before. He had thick, straight brown hair that fell down like tassels over his eyes as he sat with his head bent over a book. His skin was pale, blotchy, like sour milk, and the tortoise shell rims of his glasses stood out in ugly contrast. Every few seconds he would lick his lips, which looked dry and chapped, and then wipe them with the back of his hand. He did not look up when I came in.

I tried to remember if Lois had said anything at the last staff meeting about getting a new arrival, but as I recalled, the main topic had been Corinne's increased bedwetting. She had made no mention of a pale blond boy.

Tracy wasted no time in filling me in. "Hi, Liz," she said as soon as I walked in the door. "This is Phil. He's new. He came over the weekend on an emergency—"

The boy looked at her coldly, his blue eyes blurry behind the thick lenses of his glasses. "My name is Phil*ip*," he said. His voice was thin and shrill, and drops of saliva flew out onto the table as he spoke.

Tracy made a face. "Say it, don't spray it. We want the news, not the weather."

Philip's eyes lingered on her a moment more, the lids narrowed to small slits as though she would not be there if he could not see her, but her image must have remained, so he went back to his book. I sat down across the table from him. Looking at his tousled, shaggy hair I felt a sudden tenderness for him. I wanted him to know that I was safe. "Hi, Philip," I said. "My name is Liz."

He looked up from his book, keeping his finger at his place as a marker. "I know," he said. His face was aimed in my direction, but his eyes were focused just over my left shoulder, as though he were blind and unable to pinpoint the direction of a sound. "You're from New York and you go to Harvard. I was in New York with my mother. It's nice to meet you." His voice was patronizing, soft and high-pitched, as though I were not worth the effort it took to speak to me. As soon as he had finished his sentence, he went back to his book.

"Well, you obviously know all about me," I said. "Where are you from?"

He looked up slowly, again averting his eyes and leaving his finger where he had left off reading. "I'm originally from Pennsylvania, but we moved to Arizona when I was fairly young, so I suppose it would be more accurate to say that I am 'from' there. At least in the sense you mean." He smiled at his joke, and continued reading.

"If you ask me," said Tracy, "he's from the planet Creepo. And if you ask me, I'm sorry he wound up here."

I looked at her with what I hoped was disapproval, although I felt a giggle loose inside me. "I don't believe anyone asked you," I said. Philip did not look up from his book.

For the next few weeks, Philip spent his time as far away from us as possible, safe in his own world of Spider Man comics, nature books, *Popular Mechanics* magazines and books about clocks, calendars and the history of timekeeping. Coming to us had not been his choice, he said, he clearly did not need to be here, and he was darned if he was going to let this "little vacation with the cuckoos," as he put it, interrupt his work. He stopped reading only long enough to sleep (although he did take a book into bed with him), eat (once the staff decided that reading at the table was not permitted), and take his three daily showers. He spoke only when spoken to and laughed when any of the other kids got into trouble.

At first, it seemed that he made no trouble whatsoever himself, but soon we began to notice his unerring ability to cause trouble to erupt around him. He knew precisely what to say to provoke Franklin and Tracy to make them attack him. After each episode, he would lie on the floor, wailing and whimpering until someone came to investigate. Then he would pull himself together with righteous wrath, tell his tale of woe, and watch, his mouth turned up in a little smirk, as the perpetrator was punished. There also seemed to be a pattern to his clumsiness, a knowledge *before* he dropped the spaghetti sauce that most of it would land on Lois's white slacks, *before* he slammed the car door shut that Tracy's fingers were in the way. And yet, "It was an accident," he would say. "I'm soo, so, sorry."

As Tracy said, Philip had been a so-called emergency admit. He had been with his mother in Las Cordilleras checking out schools that he could attend when they moved there in the fall, as they had been planning to do, he told us. He had gone to the corner to buy some comics and had come back to the hotel room to find his mother dead. That was all he told us. Social services supplied the other details: that he had come back to find her lying in a pool of blood because she had shot herself in the head with a pistol and died in the time that it took him to purchase three Spider Man comic books. That there was blood everywhere, mixed with brains and flesh, his mother's head a mushy pile, her body dyed red. That Philip, not knowing what else to do, had actually held himself together well enough to call the hospital for help. That they found him there when they arrived, locked in the bathroom reading a comic, his body pressed as far back under the sink as he could get it, his head jammed against a silver pipe. That as far as they knew, she had not even left him a note. That he didn't appear to have any other relatives . . . so they sent him to Santa Clara which was low on kids anyway, since Lee and Katie had left. That was all we knew.

Throughout his first month with us, Philip tried as hard as he could to keep himself separate and, given the immediacy of his horror, we respected his needs as well as we could. He had to go to school in the morning, but he did not have to play basketball or go fishing or to the movies or participate in any other activity that he didn't want to. So he lay on his bed in the room he shared with Paul, his body curled toward the door, his head resting on his shoulder, and read, and read, and read.

Slowly, though, after a month or so of hiding in his room he began to emerge. At first it was subtle: he would take his book into the TV room in the evenings and continue to read with the book held tight against his face, surrounded by our activity, ignoring it, but allowing it to wash over him as he sat there, like waves splashing over a boulder. Every so often he would forget himself and look up from his book, peering over its edges, mutely recording the scene as the light from the ceiling flashed off the thick lenses of his glasses. As the days went by, the book was brought lower and lower, exposing first his sharp nose, then his pale, smirking lips, then his chin, down and down like an elevator, until finally his whole body was exposed, and the book lay closed and impotent in his lap.

Around that time, he also began to reach out to me, to enlist my alliance, to allow me into his world. I often wondered why he chose me, a woman, when it was a woman who had hurt him. But I was far too young to seem a mother figure to him. And I had gone to Harvard, a fact that impressed him enormously. I think he felt that, because I had that badge of intelligence, I might possibly be someone with whom he could finally have a meeting of the minds. Unfortunately, I disappointed him from the beginning.

He was sitting in the kitchen, reading, when I came in to get a snack for Paul and Corinne.

"Do you know how watches work?" he asked.

I almost dropped the jar I was carrying. In the six weeks he had been at the center, these were the first words he had spoken to anyone without being asked a direct question. "Um, no. Not really," I said. "Do you?"

"Of course. It's not terribly complicated. I'm surprised they didn't teach you that at Harvard."

I smiled. "Maybe I just didn't take the right courses. But I would like to know, now that you mention it. Do you think you could explain it to me?" Paul's fingers edged nearer the peanut butter jar and I pushed them away, praying that he wouldn't interrupt this conversation.

Philip sidestepped my question. His piercing voice rose a

little with excitement as he said, "*My* watch is quite sophisticated. Would you like to see it?"

"Sure," I said, digging heaping spoonfuls of peanut butter out of the jar and handing the spoons to Paul and Corinne, hoping it would keep them quiet for awhile. I slid in next to Philip on the bench, being careful not to crowd him. It was the closest I had ever been to him. He smelled like soap.

He focused all his attention on his watch, manipulating various buttons to show me the date, the day of the week, the calculator function, the stop watch, and the alarm. The silver of the band glinted with the ceiling light, flashing on the clear plastic face of the watch, turning it opaque, obscuring the numbers from my vision. I watched him concentrate as his fingers pushed the tiny buttons, his face flushed, the tip of his tongue pressed against the tiny hairs on his upper lip. "See?" he was saying. "You just press this button here, and . . ."

At last he was finished, and he leaned back in his chair with a satisfied expression on his face. "But the best thing," he said, "is that it is guaranteed accurate to within one-tenth of a second. For life."

"Wow, that's amazing," I said. And then, "But is it really so important not to be one-tenth of a second late for anything? I mean—"

Philip cut me off. "Yes," he said. "It is." He placed his right hand over the face of the watch protectively, shielding it from my eyes, and got up from the table, his gaze avoiding my face. His face was full of disgust and something else, an expression I couldn't place. "It is," he repeated, his voice serious, urgent. Then he turned and walked out of the room, his shoulders hunched inward, his right arm cradling his left, leaving me alone with Paul and Corinne and the smacking sound of their hungry sucking. I wondered what I had done, how I had wounded him, why he had left so abruptly, so angrily. And then I remembered, heard the voice of the pretty blond social services woman saying yes, in the time that it took him to go to the corner and back . . . Philip was right, I thought, almost hearing the words of incrimination in his brain, telling himself if I had only been there a minute earlier, a second earlier, a tenth of a second, then I might have been able to stop her, it might never have happened, it was all my fault after all. I left Paul and Corinne nursing their spoons and walked down the hall to tell Philip I was sorry, but he was reading, his body curled away from me as he lay on his bed, and he ignored me, pulling his shoulder away when I bent to touch it.

He recovered, though, proving once again Richard's dictum that just as we are powerless to cure, in our ignorance, we are powerless to kill as well. Soon after our aborted conversation, Philip started to initiate conversations with other staff. Yet with each of us, these seemed to serve not as a means of getting closer, but of keeping us at a distance. He would talk at us, reveal to us his knowledge, as if that alone would keep him safe. With all of us, these conversations went fine until he was questioned or challenged. Philip, we soon learned, needed to be right.

The first group activity he decided to join was a day trip to the pueblo in a nearby town. The summer sun beat down on us, baking the muddy earth into clay as hard and dusty as the Indian pots being hawked by old wrinkled women on all sides, and making the children hot and cranky. We wandered around the sand-colored adobe buildings, with their ladders and dark, roughly hewn windows, as Jason explained the various Indian rites and customs.

"Over here," he said, pointing to a small structure, "is the temple of the souls, where the Indians used to pray over their dead before they buried them."

"No," Philip said, shaking his head. "I hate to contradict you, Jason, but I've seen this kind of thing before. This was actually their storehouse, where they kept all the tribe's jewels and valuables that they got from raids on neighboring tribes."

Franklin, our other resident expert on all things Indian, piped up. "Uhh-uhh, man. Pueblo Indians didn't go on no raids. They didn't have jewels or nothing, either. Jason's right. This is their burial place."

Philip looked down at Franklin, the corners of his mouth turned up in disdain and flashes of fear in his eyes. Death was too dangerous a subject for him. Surely here, on an educational field trip, nothing like that could appear to frighten him. They must be wrong. And what did Franklin know, anyway? After all, he couldn't even read. Disdain won. "I'm sorry," Philip said, "but it was their storehouse."

"Was not."

"I refuse to argue about it," Philip said. "Especially with you."

"What's that supposed to mean?"

Jason had gone over to read the fact sheet, posted near the entranceway. "Ancient Temple of the souls," he read. "At this site, prayers were said over bodies of the dead before interrment. In use between—"

"I don't care what the stupid sign says," Philip whined. "Do you believe everything you read?"

I turned to Philip, falling into the same trap I so often did with him, dealing with his intellect rather than his emotions: reasoning with him. "It's okay to be wrong once in a while, you know," I said. "I'm sure that other tribes had places just like this, that they *did* use as storehouses, but in this case—"

"Okay, I was mistaken. Fine. Just forget it, will you?"

Franklin giggled. "Ha, ha. Smartass was wrong and I was right."

Philip turned on him in a fury. "Oh, yeah? Well, you're so stupid that you can't even read! I've been reading since I was a baby. Baby!"

That was too much for Franklin. He flew at Philip, punching and kicking, but before Philip had time to react, Jason and I were on them, separating them, calming them down.

I took Philip aside and stood with him in silence until his breathing became normal. "Everyone makes mistakes," I said.

"I don't."

I thought of something my mother had once told me. "Actually, making mistakes is a sign of intelligence." He snorted, just as I had done when my mother had said the same thing to me. "No, it's true," I went on. "Intelligent people use the knowledge they have to assume and predict other things. Sometimes they're wrong, but at least they're using their minds, their powers of reasoning. It's just the dummies that only recite facts all the time."

Philip took off his glasses and blew on them, his breath clouding the lenses. Then he rubbed them off on his sleeve. "Is that what they teach you at Harvard?" he asked, fitting his glasses back down on his nose.

I shrugged. "That's what they believe, anyway. Even professors aren't right all the time."

"I'm glad you told me that," he said, as we began walking back toward the bus. "Because now I know that I'm smarter than even they are."

"Huh?"

"They're wrong," he said, wiping his lips on the back of his hand. "It is important to be right. It's the most important thing in the world. That's why I am right. Almost all the time. And I was right about the storehouse, too."

"Phil-ip—"

"I was. And I'll prove it to you, too, when we get home." He boarded the van and slid in behind the driver's seat, pulling out his comic book and hiding his face between its covers. Little streams of sweat ran down the sides of his face as he turned the pages in the clammy heat, the long hairs on his arms radiant in the dusty sunshine that streamed through the window.

Philip's need to be right about facts was surpassed only by his need to seek out and predict the disasters of daily life before they happened; thus, he soon became our resident prophet of doom. If we had a fishing trip scheduled, Philip knew it would rain, he was sure of it. If it didn't rain, and we went on the trip, Philip would sit in the front of the van, just behind the driver, his eyes fastened on the dashboard, and swear that we were going to run out of gas, he knew it. If Jason showed him that we had a full tank, then Philip would whimper that the gas gauge was broken, or, more likely, that the whole van was falling apart—how old was it anyway, what year, how many miles—and we were going to break down and probably be stranded forever. If we got to the fishing site without a mishap, he would refuse to handle any of the equipment and would instead sit on a blanket drinking his juice and predict between sips that someone's eye would get poked out by a hook, that Corinne would fall into the water and drown, that the mayonnaise on the tunafish sandwiches was spoiled from sitting in the sun and we'd probably all get food poisoning and have to be rushed to the hospital. And if none of that happened, if we got through the day intact and in relative peace, all of his car worries would reappear, with no less intensity, on the ride home.

"Hey, let me do the worrying. You just relax and enjoy the ride," I would say, when I was driving. Or when that didn't work, which it rarely did, I would try to work through with him the worst-possible-case scenario. "Okay, Philip. Look. We're not going to run out of gas [or break down or crash or get a flat tire]. But even if we did, what would be the worst that could happen?"

"We could be stranded," he'd whine, his leg bouncing up and down.

"Well, probably a car would come along sooner or later and help us. But even if one didn't, what would be the worst that could happen?"

He sighed heavily and chewed on a hangnail. "We could starve to death by the side of the road."

"But if we didn't come back by evening, the other staff would know that something was wrong. I wrote down our route in the log book, so they could always find us."

"We could get hit by a car by the side of the road, and we could die because there would be no way to get to the hospital." His voice rose in fear.

"Oh, I'd make sure you all stayed far back from the road. I'd keep you safe."

"Hmmmmmmm," he'd say at last, settling back in his seat. And then, anxiously: "Hey, Liz, are you sure we have enough gas? I think we're going to run out of gas." And the whole routine would start again.

Of course once he'd shown them this Achilles' heel, the other kids teased him mercilessly. "Oh, no!" Franklin would say, mock terror in his voice. "Did you feel that bump? *Chingasa,* man! I bet the axle got cracked on that one for sure!"

Philip would look at him in terror, falling for it every time. "Do you really think so?"

And Franklin and the rest of the kids (and sometimes the staff, as well, depending on how long and how nerve-racking the trip had been, and how many times Philip had predicted that we weren't going to make it) would erupt in helpless laughter.

But Philip was above vengence, or so he said. "I abhor physical violence of any kind," he told Franklin, when the latter had called him a wussy because he wouldn't fight back. "An intelligent person should be able to retaliate just with words."

But he did get even with them, in his own, subtle way, and not always just with words.

"Ouch!" Franklin yelled, looking up from his cereal one morning at breakfast. "That hurt, man!" He pointed at Philip. "He stepped on my foot."

"I'm sorry," Philip said. "I guess I'm clumsy early in the morning."

I poured Philip some cereal and a glass of juice and set them down in front of him. Tracy appeared in the doorway, looking tousled and cranky. "Hi," she said. "What's for breakfast?"

"Just cold cereal and fruit today, hon," I said. "Sorry, but we got kind of a late start."

Tracy scowled and slid onto the bench next to Philip. He turned to look at her. "You, for example, are seventeen minutes late. We're supposed to be at breakfast by eight, and it's eight seventeen. And thirty seconds."

"Fuck you," Tracy said under her breath.

I gave Tracy her cereal. "Tracy knows the schedule, Phil," I said. "You just take care of yourself, and let her take care of herself."

"But I'm just trying to help her not to get into trouble, the way she usually does."

"That's not your job. You just keep yourself out of trouble, okay?"

"Whatever you say." There now, that was easy enough, I thought. But as Franklin and I began to talk about the day's activities, Philip edged his undrunk juice closer and closer to Tracy, without her noticing, until it lay directly between her hand and the sugar bowl. Sure enough, when Tracy reached for the sugar, as she did every morning, the juice spilled all over the table, much of it landing in her lap.

Tracy jumped up, dumping the bench and Philip onto the floor. "Asshole," she yelled at Philip. "You put that there on purpose."

Philip looked at her in amazement. "Don't yell at me just because *you* spilled the juice!"

"You better clean it up."

"*I'm* not going to clean it up. Whoever spills it, cleans it. That's the rule. You spilled it, you clean it."

Tracy shoved him down, making sure he fell into the puddle.

"Liz!" he yelled. "Did you see that?"

"How could I have missed it?" I asked him, marvelling at how well he had succeeded once again at getting Tracy in trouble, at making himself the victim so that someone else could be the criminal and take the rap. I was often surprised by Philip's compulsion to be the victim. It seemed to me that he had played that role often enough in real life that it should have worn thin here at the RTC. But it was a role in which he felt comfortable. As long as he could set the scene, place the juice, provoke the punch, he could still be in control, and as long as he was in control, nothing could ever hurt him more than he was capable of bearing. It was a perfect way to get rid of his anger, to act out his rage, without ever being responsible for its consequences. After all, as he so often reminded us after one of these episodes, it wasn't *his* fault.

I stood there, surveying the sticky scene, Philip and Tracy both dripping orange juice, and wondered what I should do. If I punished Tracy, I would be playing directly into Philip's hands. On the other hand, if I didn't punish her, I would be condoning her use of violence, her loss of control, and at the same time allowing Philip to feel doubly victimized. And if I punished Philip, he would like that best of all. I decided not to punish anyone, to treat the entire thing like the accident Philip claimed it was. "Tracy," I said, "go to your room and put on some dry clothes. Philip, here are some paper towels."

"But—"

"I don't care whose fault it was. Just clean it up."

He looked pained. "Tracy pushed me into the juice. Aren't you going to punish her?"

"Just clean up the floor. Please."

"But I didn't spill it—"

"I know, Phil. Just clean it up, okay?"

"But that's not fair!"

"Philip!" My voice was sharper than I had intended. He took the paper towels and swirled them around in the puddle, spraying the juice in a wider circle on the floor, making sure that a few drops landed on the cuffs of my jeans. He muttered to himself but I ignored him. "Thank you, Philip," I said when he was done.

I brought the incident up at the staff meeting that afternoon, and the room was suddenly alive with examples, each of the staff needing to vent his frustration about this impossible kid who, for example:

"Slammed my finger in a drawer, by accident," said Joan.

"Almost sliced my finger off when he was cutting up an onion, by accident," said Lois.

"Managed to spill his water twice and drop his fork three times when I took him out to eat last week, by accident," said Bernie.

"Always has to contradict absolutely everything I say," David said. It was the first time I had ever heard him express exasperation about any of the kids.

In fact, when they got to talking about him, none of the staff really *liked* Philip. They felt sorry for him, of course, and tried to help him in every way they could, but he was so devious, so petulant, such a pain in the ass, Bernie said, that it was really impossible to like him.

I liked him, though. Of all the kids, he was the first one I felt that I truly understood. I thought about him a lot: about how it would feel to walk into a hotel room one day and find that your mother had abandoned you forever, with a bullet through her head. I thought about the anger, and the fear, and the relief, too, mingled in because she must have been a deeply troubled woman, not the easiest to live with, and then the guilt he must have felt, the overwhelming terror of being all, all alone. I remembered one day coming home from school to an empty house and imagining that my mother had died. There was a pot bubbling on the stove and the front door was ajar, I knew she would be back in a few minutes, but the fear that she was gone forever even then in the warm, familiar kitchen had made my throat tighten, my eyes tear. I thought about the insanity that Philip must have dancing around his ears, as voices in the air crooned to him, "It's your fault, you made her do it, you drove her to do it, she did it herself she left I hate her she's my mother I can't hate her I love her and she loves me but if she loves me then how could she go and leave me all alone . . ." With a life that unsure, that chaotic, I thought, I would also want to control everything I possibly could, would want to measure the seconds as they went by, the only sure and constant strand in the hopelessly tangled skein, would need to be right about all the facts I could, facts as friends, because anything else would be too dangerous. And I too would try to see all that could go wrong before it did. I would want nothing to surprise me, ever again.

I did not know whether anyone could go through that and survive, could be healed, made whole again after seeing all that he had seen. Yet I sometimes dreamed that there might be some hope for him, because with it all, with all that he had suffered, he had not, I thought, lost his capacity to feel, to empathize, to care. No matter how much he provoked Tracy and Franklin and the farm kids, he was unfailingly kind to people and things weaker than he. Unlike many of the other kids, he never tortured the animals, and he was always nice, almost tender, to Paul, with whom he shared a room. Or so it seemed.

Then one night when I went to check on the kids after having tucked them all in, I found Philip in bed with Paul. He lay in Paul's bed, forcing the helpless, autistic boy to move his hand up and down on Philip's penis. I stood frozen in the doorway, my hand clutching the knob, feeling oddly betrayed. Jesus, no, Philip, I thought. Philip was completely absorbed, his head thrown back, sweaty against the pure white of the pillow. I felt shocked and embarrassed, but also fascinated, watching Paul's hand move up and down, up and down as he moaned his noise, ouiouiouiouiouioui. I wondered if he knew the difference between moving his hand on Philip's penis and pumping the handle of the toy top that he loved to watch spin. I wondered how many times they had done this, and whether it explained what now appeared to be Philip's loverlike behavior toward Paul. Did Philip threaten him to keep him from "telling"? Or did he merely rely on Paul's illness, his craziness, as one relies on a dog's muteness when one enlists him as a confessor? As Paul looked up and saw me in the doorway a flash of anger went across his face. He kept up the rhythm of his hand, but his noises changed from ouiouioui to the high-pitched shriek he used when he was upset. I did not know whether he was angry at me for discovering them, or was voicing his anger at Philip for forcing him to do something he hated. The shriek sliced through the air, a clean line dividing the room in half. I saw Philip's pain and guilt and need on one side, and Paul's on the other, and I stood there, balancing on the edge.

"Philip," I said. His head jerked up and he looked both guilty and fearful. Naked, he jumped out of Paul's bed and bolted the few steps across the room into his own, pulling the rumpled covers up over his body.

"I was just tucking him in," he said.

I have never wished so much that I were a man. If I were a man, I would have known how to wink or smile knowingly and say, It's okay, kiddo, we all go through it, it's all right.

Or I would have known how to clap him on the shoulder so that he need not hate himself for his needs along with everything else, and say I understood what he was feeling and that it was all right, but not now, and not with Paul. My breasts felt heavy, sagging against my chest. I could say the same things, but like a mother who has found her adolescent son masturbating and wants to assure him it is perfectly natural, no guilt, I knew the tone of my voice, my disgust, my embarrassment, my own self-conscious sexuality would betray me. There was nothing I could do.

"No," I said at last, as calmly as I could, my arms folded across my chest. "You were making Paul masturbate you." Philip's face flushed red but I continued, trying to keep my voice neutral. "You know, masturbation is a perfectly normal thing. It's normal to have sexual feelings and it's normal for you to want to deal with some of those feelings by masturbating." I took a deep breath. "But Paul has no way of telling you how he feels about what you're doing. He may feel uncomfortable or trapped or angry or scared, and he would have no way of telling you. He is really defenseless. And it's not fair of you to force him to—"

"I wasn't forcing him. He wanted to."

"We really have no way of knowing that," I said. "That's why sex play between any of you kids is absolutely against the rules."

Philip licked his lips and shrugged. "Okay," he said at last. He took out a comic book and began to read, his eyes hidden by the cover.

I went over to Paul. He was rocking in his bed. I reached out and stroked his shoulder gently, telling him it was okay, that Philip was not going to touch him anymore, that it was going to be all right. He shrank slightly from my touch, and kept rocking. I needed to leave. "Now go to sleep," I said, feeling inadequate. "Both of you. I'll see you in the morning." I left the room, leaving the door wide open.

Philip was a little bit afraid of me after that, I think. Instead of teasing me, as he'd begun doing, he now fed me compliments, as though I knew a terrible secret and would tell it if he did anything to cross me. I tried to tell him a couple of times that it wasn't true, tried to talk about his feelings, tried to enter his world with him, but he would only talk to me about the future, and only in terms of time.

"Hey Liz," he said. "Do you want to see how long I can hold my breath?"

One day, on an impulse, I gave Philip an old-fashioned watch with a round face and only two hands: one for the hours, which were marked off by numbers lying all around its face, and one for minutes, which weren't marked at all. I don't think he liked it very much. Someday, perhaps, he will.

James

James spoke with twisting fingers. He would sit at the kitchen table for hours, watching the little birds that only he could see play as they hovered over the burners on the stove, or he would stare transfixed at the light sockets on the wall, suddenly blinking and laughing, hauntingly, the rhythm of his fingers quickening. James Bunyon, Bunyon-Sonyon. Tall and thin, pale and brittle, like an icicle dangling from a rod, thawing as the year wore on towards summer, only to freeze as winter neared again.

James was brilliant. In his more lucid moments he could perform complex math problems in his head, or draw sketches and pictures whose beauty was not diminished by the fact that he would use only black and white. Yet day after day, as I worked with him in the schoolroom, the sheets of math problems I gave him would come back with all the answers correct but, barely discernible under the lines of minute writing he had painstakingly printed above, an endless refrain—like but love not love and like but you are not love is love but like not is not like and like like love—line after line, filling the page.

James's history was hazy. He had been adopted by Mr. and Mrs. Bunyon, who already had two children, both girls and considerably older, when he was about four years old. By the time James was twelve, Mr. Bunyon had died and both sisters had moved away, leaving James alone with his adoptive mother. Mrs. Bunyon was not an evil woman. She loved James, or said she did. But she had a life-style to maintain, a need to have everything just so, a place for everything and everything in its place, and no place for a tall, lanky, unhappy boy. Her house, in which she had raised three children, was decorated entirely in white: the walls were white, the furniture was white, even the carpeting was a thick, luxurious white shag. She was apparently devastated by her husband's death and her emotional resources were such that she was unable to cope with her increasingly strange and difficult son, who insisted on defecating daily, directly in the middle of the white shag rug.

Frustrated and hopeless, Mrs. Bunyon finally took him to the town mental health clinic, where the diagnosis was unanimous and swift: schizophrenic reaction-type, mixed, undifferentiated, chronic. And so James came to Santa Clara.

When I first met him, James was a shadow. Pale and silent most of the time, when he did speak it was in a murmur so low and so obviously painful that I felt cruel asking him to talk to me. Sometimes in the evenings he would join me and the other kids in games of backgammon or checkers, moving his pieces with three fingers wound tightly around each other, hesitantly, afraid both to lose and to win. More often, though, he would just sit by himself, staring into the patterns his fingers made as he twisted them around and around, or watching birds and monsters and fairies that only he could see, laughing at their antics or widening his eyes in terror at their threats.

"What is it, James?" we would ask him, touching him gently on the shoulder or leg to announce our presence. But all we would get for an answer was an unearthly laugh, from far, far away.

One cold night in February, when I went to tuck him in to bed, he wasn't there. No one knew where he was, none of the kids had seen him. Panicked, we searched the house; it was not like James to run away, and in the back of our minds, we were all terrified of finding him somewhere, dead. He was not in the house. I ran outside, calling his name over and over, telling him that we loved him and wanted him to come back, that we were not angry, we just wanted him back. Then suddenly there he was, a pale, naked ghost in the moonlight, walking in the field next to the house, around and around in a wide circle.

"James!" I said, my breath coming out in wisps of steam in the winter air. I ran to him. "Hi, there," I said.

"Hi."

"What are you doing?"

"I don't know."

"Aren't you cold?"

"Yes."

"Well, why don't you come back inside now, and put some clothes on."

"Okay."

"If you want to go for a walk, you should tell someone where you're going, okay?"

He laughed, a sheepish little laugh, as if to say to me that telling someone would have pretty much defeated the purpose, that he was nearly eighteen years old, after all, and that he shouldn't have to tell anyone when he wanted to go for a walk, but that he knew that we were stronger and in charge, and he certainly wasn't about to fight. "Okay," he said.

"Otherwise we worry about you, you know?"

"Yes."

He laughed again, and let me lead him gently back to the house.

He frightened me, this tall, vacant boy. Beneath his craziness, under his sad little laugh, beyond his empty stare, he seemed to know so much, to understand all my little lies and tricks and foibles, to see into my soul. But he looked so lost as he sat there, twisting his brittle, rigid fingers, and his contained rage was so palpable behind his gentle laugh when the other kids teased him that I found myself drawn to him in spite of myself. He was like a complicated jigsaw puzzle with hundreds of tiny pieces, like his mother's house decorated all in white, and I always felt with him that I could never fit them together correctly.

Once, for instance, shortly after I'd begun working at the center, I stumbled into a living-room scene where Richard was wrestling with James on the floor, tickling him. Remembering my own childhood, my father tickling my brother and me, I immediately jumped in, saying, "C'mon, James, let's get him." But as soon as I got into the act, James retreated, crawling onto a chair to watch the action. Richard told me later, his anger undisguised, that he had been trying to get James to express some hostility, and had gotten him just about to the breaking point when I had ruined it with, as he put it, in his crisp Australian accent, my "fun and games rubbish." For a long time after that, whenever James laughed his eerie laugh, it was hard not to feel that he was laughing at me.

Winter lingers a long time in the mountains of the Southwest, but as the days grew longer, and the first buds blossomed, we all noticed a change in James. At first, the difference was subtle. I was eating breakfast with the kids one Saturday morning. They had all been good, so I had cooked some bacon as a special treat. Tracy finished hers first, as usual, and asked for seconds, but it had all been given out already.

She noticed that James still had a piece left on his plate.

"Hey, James, can I have your bacon?" she said, reaching across Philip to grab it for herself.

"No," said James in a low voice.

She paid no attention, stuffing the bacon into her mouth. "Thanks," she said.

I was horrified. That was the first time I had ever heard James protest anyone else's actions, and here he was finding out that it didn't do any good after all. "Tracy!" I snapped. "James said no. He wanted to eat it himself."

Tracy swallowed her mouthful. "Oh, he was just kidding. Weren't you, James?"

James looked down at his empty plate. "Yes," he mumbled. "Do you want more bacon?" I asked him. "Tracy was wrong to grab like that, so I'll gladly make you some more."

"No," he said.

"Oh, c'mon. You can have it if you want it." He shook his head and laughed softly, retreating back into himself.

"I'll take some more," said Franklin.

"Moah! Moah! Moah!" echoed Paul, banging on his plate. But from James, nothing.

As he began to emerge as a person, I saw that James had quite a good, if bitter, sense of humor. One day at lunch, about a month later, Tracy said that she was stuffed.

"I wish you were stuffed and mounted," James said. Franklin giggled.

"What did you say?" asked Tracy, her face flushed.

"Nothing."

"Hey, good for you, James," said Richard, laughing so hard he nearly choked on his food. "That was pretty funny."

Little by little, as the summer wore on, he opened up in other ways as well. He still twirled his fingers, but he held them a little less rigidly. He began to seem more interested in the people and conversations around him than in the burners of the stove or the light sockets. When he laughed now, it was likely to be because of something funny in our world, rather than his. He seemed freer, happier, less haunted, and more willing to accept the fact that he existed here and now, to feel that he had a right to the time and space he occupied. Instead of slinking along the walls when he walked, he now, sometimes, dared to move through the center of the room.

Having heard through James's mother that he had once been an excellent roller skater, Richard and I took him to the rink in town and told him to give it a whirl.

"I can't."

"Oh, sure you can. It's like riding a bicycle. Once you know how, you never forget."

"I can't ride a bicycle," James said, clearly conscious that he was making a joke. We pressed our advantage, then strapped him and ourselves into our skates, and off we went. I am a terrible roller skater, a complete klutz, so for the first five minutes it was all I could do to keep myself from falling. I finally remembered the rhythm, though, and called out to James that I would be right with him, only to see him go sailing by on the inside track. If he wasn't gliding like a pro, well, at least he was aware of all the parts of his body, completely in tune.

In his awakening, James became more aware of the staff and grew to feel that he was perhaps entitled to some of their time and attention. He might ask in his hesitant, halting voice if I would play a game of backgammon with him, if Richard would take him skating, if Bernie would cook him an omelette, if Jason would tell him a story. It was as if he had never before realized that he could influence the events around him merely by opening his mouth. But asking for favors is not the same as forming a relationship. To him, the staff still seemed as gods, benevolent now but still omnipotent, dispensing favors or punishments from on high, and the rest of the kids had been his tormentors for too long to consider any of them friends. But then he discovered Franklin.

Franklin, infinitely gentle with animals and people who were weaker than he, soon became James's roommate, his self-appointed protector and, eventually, his friend. Although Franklin often confided to us in private that James was "a little bit crazy," he was the soul of compassion to James himself. "Hey, lighten up, man!" he would say if he saw James withdrawing, or staring in horror out into space. "Come see the arrowhead I found." And off they would go.

"Hey, James, listen to this," and Franklin would launch into another of his grandmother's tales, as James listened, his eyes focused, his face alive.

With Franklin by his side, James felt secure enough to be brave. "No!" he'd say, his voice quavering but authoritative, when he was watching television and Philip or Tracy came in and changed the channel. "Leave it alone. I was watching that." Shocked, they would usually comply, and when they didn't, Franklin would make sure that one of the staff heard about it, and that James stuck up for his rights. For Franklin's sense of justice, if not always of right and wrong, was absolute.

As he relaxed, James also dared to be bad, to be mischievous. He invented little hide and seek games to play with the staff, especially when we were in a hurry to get somewhere. Where's James, we would say, all loaded into the van, and then we would have to go back to the house and hunt for him, until we eventually found his tall frame stuffed under a bed or inside a crowded closet, his face pressed into the coats. Later, he would jump out at us from his hiding places before we found him, whispering "Boo!" and laughing until he doubled over, unable to contain himself.

What filled me with such joy, and such sorrow, was not James's sudden willingness to assert his strength, but rather his increasing ability to show weakness. In this, too, he was helped by Franklin. Franklin was eleven years old. He still had his childhood roundness, and with his flashing smile and propensity for throwing his arms around anyone and everyone to express either joy or sorrow, he collected far more than his share of cuddling and caressing. James, on the other hand, was a gangly, pimply seventeen, far taller than I, who had only recently begun to remain "in" his flesh when it was touched. But towards the end of summer, I often noticed him staring at us when I went to cuddle Franklin, or let him climb into my lap while I rocked him or tucked him into bed at night. In his hunger, James began to act like Franklin. Smiling a small smile, the six-foot-tall, sweaty manchild would try to climb into my lap, would put out his arms to give Jason a hug and end by touching him lightly on the back, would stumble purposely into Richard when they went roller skating, or shyly lock their fingers together, mutely asking for the simple human contact that he had denied himself, or that had been denied him, all these years.

One still night, toward the end of August, I was putting James and Franklin to bed. I read them a few chapters of *Stuart Little*, about his yachting race, and told them that I lived right near the pond where it all happened. Then I went over to Franklin's bed and lifted the sheet up high, letting it drift down slowly over his legs, giving the illusion of a breeze in the warm room. I tucked the sheet in around him and kissed him goodnight on both cheeks and his forehead, watching James watch us, longing and jealousy plain in his eyes.

Straightening, I said to Franklin, as I did every night, "Good night, sleep tight, see you in the morning light."

"Do not let the bedbugs bite," he answered.

Then I went over to James's side of the room. For as long as I had known him, James had always felt particularly vulnerable in bed and hated to be touched when he was prone. But that night, the wanting in his eyes was so great that I asked him if he wanted to be tucked in. He nodded, and I went through all the steps I had with Franklin. He flinched a little when I kissed him, but kept his hand firmly on my arm and smiled.

"Good night, sleep tight, see you in the morning light," I said.

"Do not let the bedbugs bite," he answered.

In September, James turned eighteen. Beyond the cake and presents, there was the reality that our center was supposed to be for short-term cases only, six- to twelve-month confinements, eighteen months at the outside, and was supposed to treat only minors. James was now breaking the rules on both counts: he had been there almost two years and, in the eyes of the law, this teenager who crawled into my lap to be rocked was now an adult. "What to do with James" became the overriding topic of conversation among the staff.

"He's doing so well now," Richard said at one meeting. "How about trying some kind of group home? Maybe a sheltered workshop or something."

Jason was doodling on a yellow pad. "I don't know," he said. "James is doing great now, but it's summer . . . what if he loses it again, like he did last fall? He'd never make it in a group home then."

"Aren't you the pessimist," Richard said. "I think it's different this time. I think he's really getting better."

"Maybe."

"What we really need," I said, "is to place him somewhere in South America, where it never gets cold." Everyone laughed, and the decision was once again put off for another day.

As summer hardened into fall, however, James solved the

problem for us. Little by little all the gains he'd made over the past months slipped away. He stopped smiling when I tucked him in, then he pulled away, then he just lay there, making me feel that I was tucking a log into the bed. He still suffered himself to be taken roller skating but would creep along the edge of the railing, clutching it tight, staring at his feet to make sure that they were still there. Again he would sit and rock for hours, staring with glassy eyes out the window towards the mountains, and even Franklin could not drag him out of himself. Finally, around November, as all of us watched with breaking hearts, he again became transfixed by stove burners and light sockets, laughing softly to himself as he stared his wide-eyed stare. In vain we pleaded with him to come back to us, to give us a hug, to roll in the leaves, to play a game. At first he would respond, but with more and more apathy, until finally, as before, all he would say was "Okay," "Maybe," and "I don't care."

Hard as it was to watch all this, we would gladly have kept him with us, where at least he seemed unlikely to get worse, but we were already under pressure to get him up and out.

Miraculously, it was discovered that one of James's sisters lived in Southern California. We were sure that if we could just find a way to send him there, to play out his life in the warmth of the sun, that he would be fine. It seemed to us to be the perfect solution. Unfortunately, his sister did not agree. Oh, she cared about him, of course. She said she'd love to help any way she could, that James could visit any time he liked, but that she just didn't feel able to assume full responsibility for him right now—she had just begun starting her own family—and she hoped we understood.

We did understand. But there was nothing that either Dan

Johnson or Lois could do to keep him a day longer. And so James, passive and withdrawn, was returned to his mother's white house.

The day James left, I sat at the kitchen table and stared at the clock that hung above the stove. I watched the second hand brush by the numbers on the face, rushing down past one and two to six, then slowly climbing back up to twelve, only to fall again. I thought of Sisyphus, wondering what would happen if once, just for a moment, the seconds stopped, if Sisyphus triumphed over the rock and forced it over the top, or gave up on it entirely and let it tumble down the mountain unpursued. Would the world end? Or would it just float forever? I wondered if James knew the answer.

Paul

Rudolph the red-nosed reindeer
had a very shiny nose,
and if you ever saw it
you would even say it glows.

We sang as Paul rocked back and forth, back and forth, clutching his torn, faded copy of the storybook Rudolph to his chest. I sang; he snapped his mouth open and shut, and murmured ouiouiouiouioui. Sometimes he flapped his hand, the fingers loose and extended, flickering up and down in front of his face. Sometimes he squeezed his stiffened fingers together and placed the tips close to his mouth, screeching with all his might. Sometimes he blinked his eyes open and shut, a hundred times a minute, filtering out all that he did not want to see.

All of the other reindeer
used to laugh and call him names.
They never let poor Rudolph
join in any reindeer games.

I sang to him as we walked along the country roads together, Paul always several paces behind, propelling himself along on his toes, pausing sometimes to crouch and fondle a leaf, sometimes to leap as high as he could, over and over, like a pogo stick, yelling at the top of his lungs, sometimes to screech, sometimes just to sit and rock. He would pick up a twig and stare at it, holding it close to his eye, reaching out with a curled tongue as if to draw it into his mouth.

Then one foggy Christmas Eve,
Santa came to say
"Rudolph with your nose so bright
won't you guide my sleigh tonight?"

I sang our song to Paul as he lay in the playroom, draped like a wet towel over a huge red bouncing ball, rolling slowly across the floor. Once in a great while he would crawl into my lap to be rocked, his long legs hanging lifeless over mine, his back slumped against my chest. I would lower my voice, whispering my warm breath into his ears as his fingers, like those of a blind person, explored the contours of my face. Once, his finger slid into my mouth, and I kissed it gently as I sang.

Then how the reindeer loved him
as they shouted out with glee:
"Rudolph the red-nosed reindeer
you'll go down in history."

I do not know what the song meant to him. He was never able to tell me, and I was never able to get far enough into his world to figure it out. It was a strange world, full of rage and hurt and betrayal, full of terror, full of life, and of the will to live, to be, despite, to spite, the people who had cast him into nonbeing. It was a world in which objects were people, to be played with, to love, to hate, to hurt, and people merely objects, tools, who existed only to help him obtain his most minimal physical needs. In Paul's world, other people had no part. He had cast them out, as he had been cast out. What need did he have of us, when his world was filled with so much else? He could look at a tiny fluff of dust for hours, holding it to his mouth or nose or cheek, loving it, studying it, knowing it to its very essence, but could sit in a room with me for hours and never once look at my face.

Paul's was a world that was wholly his. In it, he was the sun, the center of gravity around which we all existed as so much matter. In it, he could make us all nonexistent, as those in our world had so successfully done with him. Yet it was not a happy world nor a peaceful one, for our world kept intruding, asking things of him that he was mortally frightened of giving, and offering things that he could not allow himself to take. He peopled his world with strange noises and visions to be seen through flickering fingers, like actors in front of a strobe, but we were there as well, I was there, singing to him as we sat together in the sunny, still playroom. We would not let him not be.

Our trespasses filled him with rage. He had worked so hard all those years to strike the dangerous balance between nonexistence and actual death, had removed himself from the world in which he was not wanted, only to be told by us that he was wanted after all—he, Paul, the fourteen-year-old boy with slanted eyes and a pointed nose, when he knew down to the core of his being that no such person existed any longer.

His eyes were deep green, flecked with gold and brown and blue, but cloudy, like a smoldering volcano, always ready to erupt. It was difficult to see the eyes, to catch them watching. Usually he hid them behind a book or a toy or his fluttering lids. But sometimes, if you looked stealthily, you could see through his rocking, watch him watching you, his eyes a steady gleam of cold green light. Eyes that looked through rather than at you, seeing, knowing all. Oh, he was angry, such rage and hate inside the eyes, lit with a light so cold it burned, like dry ice. Medusa eyes, I used to think, as if eyes could really turn people to stone, as if they had turned him to stone already, a stone statue rocking dangerously on a high pedestal. His eyes seemed filled with intelligence, too, and my God, Paulie, I used to think, what might you have been. He was tall and thin and strong, but he moved hesitantly, with a shuffling gait, like someone who had just learned to walk. A fourteen-year-old toddler. I don't think I ever saw him run. He had pale, creamy skin and long dark lashes and a face as thin and chiseled as a deer. A reindeer.

When Paul was four years old and his sister Corinne nearly three, they had both been locked in a small room, perhaps a closet, from which they were not let out for the next seven years. Their brother, Peter, had the daily job of changing the shoe box they used as a toilet and bringing them their food. With rare exceptions, he was the only person they ever saw. For seven years. How many days is seven years? How many hours? How many minutes, sitting in the dark? How long would you cry, a four-year-old child, before you knew that no one would ever answer? How long could you keep crying after you knew? And what would you do when the crying had stopped, when the world was empty, and you were too young yet to have a self to fill it up? What would you think about, a four-year-old child, alone with a baby sister in the dark of a tiny room? Surely you would know that they had abandoned you, your mother, your father, that they had left your soul to die. Would you hear the noises of the family at dinner below? Would you listen to the sounds of your brothers and sisters, playing free throughout the house? Would you be old enough, a four-year-old child, to wonder why you were the one? Could you reason that it must be the badness within you? Could you kill yourself as your body sat there, breathing, second after second, filling up the days of seven years?

Paul had done nothing so very crazy, after all. In a way, he had only done what he had been told to do, like any four-year-old, anxious to please. Told by his parents not to be, he had ceased to be in their world; he had imploded like a black hole, all his energies surging inward. I used to lie in bed at night, staring through the dark at the ceiling, counting the layers of air above my head in the grainy light and trying to be that child, building his own world in the confines of a three-by-four closet. I could never do it. But then, it had taken Paul years and years.

I used to wonder, sometimes, how it could have happened. What could the parents have told the other children? There were three older children and a younger brother and sister, all of whom were sent to school each day. What must the parents have told them to keep them from mentioning the fact that, oh, yeah, and by the way, I've got this other brother and sister, see, but my folks keep them locked up at home. Why were Paul and Corinne singled out for the torture? How could the parents have done it, have lived with themselves? I had been told that it was the mother who had done it, really. That she had been the jailer, the one to lock them up and throw away the key while the father just watched, inert, pretending, perhaps, that the children had died. I did not see much difference, could not fathom whose culpability was the greater. My son is dead, he might have told himself, the father, might even have been told by his wife one night at dinner, perhaps, over the green beans. Surely, though, somewhere within himself, he must have known.

And what of the mother? I tried to empathize, to understand. Alone and afraid, shut up in a house with five young children, the youngest, Paul and Corinne, born so close together, both sickly children, I had been told. Maybe one day she just wished that they would disappear, shut them in a closet because they would not stop screaming and her head was aching and the older kids were begging for a story. And once she had put them there, in the closet, had locked them in and ignored their frightened wails, how could she ever let them out? In the closet, they became embodiments of her evil, for what mother could do that to her own children? Of necessity she blocked them out of her mind, literal skeletons, to be forgotten, buried, denied. They stopped screaming, they stopped existing, of course, they had never existed at all. And she went on with her life, the life of her family, had two more children, a boy and a girl, oh, aren't they sweet, and nurtured them until they grew whole and ripe, quite forgetting the fetid fruit that rotted like a carton of forgotten apples in a tiny room in the back of the house.

But it was impossible to fathom.

No real way to understand, either, how the ordeal had finally ended. Perhaps it never would have ended except that one day Paul got out and ran naked down the street with a terrified Peter at his heels. Social services moved in then, began asking questions, interviewing the other children, talking to Peter. Finally, upon subsequent investigation and after months of red tape, all seven children were removed from the home and placed in the foster custody of Dan Johnson. The parents were permanently enjoined from ever seeing Paul or Corinne again, but they were given visiting rights for the other children.

When Paul emerged from the closet, he was a wild child. Silent and still, he would sit and rock for hours in the same spot on the floor, like a caged bird suddenly set free, digging his claws into his familiar perch. I had read that kittens raised in the dark lose the ability to see, and grope pitifully, bumping into walls even in brightly lit rooms. Paul reminded me of such a kitten, frightened, blind, unwilling to give up the safety of his little world for the overwhelming demands of our big one. He could not talk, made almost no sounds at all, at first, although there was nothing the matter with his vocal chords, no neurological damage that anyone could find. Perhaps he had simply lost faith in the power of speech. He also seemed to understand almost nothing of what was said to him, staring stony-eyed past all offers of juice, play, hugs, cookies. When he was hungry, he would grab an adult arm and move it to an apple or box of raisins, which would then be handed to him. He could not use a fork or spoon, was not toilet trained, could not dress himself. And yet, there was something there, behind the cloudy film that obscured the eyes, a life-force lurking in the shadows, flashing like the beam from a lighthouse, beckoning, begging don't give up on me. Not yet.

He would spend his days in endless motion, rocking on the floor, snapping his hand shut with a sharp popping sound that no one else was able to imitate, chasing miniscule bits of dust that danced in the streams of sunlight through the windows, beating rhythmically on the floor with a stray Lincoln log or backgammon piece from somebody else's forgotten game, or just staring through his flickering fingers, eyes unfocused, head turned toward the wall. When he was angry, he would place stiffened hands against his face, so that the tips of his fingers just touched his lips, press his face in close, shutting his eyes to make the person disappear.

The days passed, days into months, months into years, and slowly Paul gave in to some of the demands that our world made on him. Uncomprehendingly, he learned that shitting in the toilet would earn him a cookie or a couple of grapes, while shitting in his pants would not. That stripping off his clothes and running naked through the house would provoke angry shouts, perhaps strong arms wrapped around him, pressing his nose into a corner, but putting legs into pants and arms into shirt sleeves in the morning might get him an extra helping of cereal and a soft touch on his head. That pointing to the food he wanted and moaning "moah, moah, moah" might get him what he wanted, while moving an adult arm toward a box would more likely produce a terse, "Ask for it, Paul." He was smart. He learned. By the time I got to the center, he spent his days rocking quietly, alone in the corner with a torn book clutched to his chest, staring out furtively from lowered eyelids as the noisy life of the center bustled on around him and snapping his mouth shut with the senseless rhythm of a frog catching flies. And, oh, they told me, how much better he had gotten!

Paul learned other things, too. I watched them teach him. In the schoolhouse each morning with his sweet, pretty teacher, he learned to trace the letters of the alphabet in a long flat box filled with sand, and to push square blocks through square holes and round blocks through round ones. He got so he could do it all by himself, and his teacher was happy. He learned to bounce on a red rubber ball, his too-long legs bunched up against its sides, as he watched himself, embarrassed, in the large mirrors in the playroom. He learned to look at television, quietly, whenever it was on, his fingers flickering against the patterns of light on the screen, to sit quietly, to rock quietly in a corner through rest period, or when the other kids were acting up.

Anger, he learned, was a bad thing, at least in the way that he expressed it. "No, Paul!" they would yell at him when he pressed his hands against his face and began to screech. "No! Be quiet!" they would say, tearing his hands away from his face, hissing at him, threatening him with the time-out space, or sometimes, if he would not stop, pressing his face into a corner until he was finally quiet and good.

And still, they had not killed him. Still the light was there, like the sirens' call: come to me, come to me.

But maybe the light, like the call of the sirens, was itself only a trap. Beckoning from within, it suggested a prisoner, weak, frail perhaps, yet otherwise whole and sound, held captive against his will behind thick enemy walls. It is so easy, watching these children, to believe in that prisoner, the myth of rescue. But it is not so simple. The prison and the captive are both aspects of the child, inseparable. There are walls to be broken down, but they are walls which the child himself has created, and may struggle to buttress, fighting your attempts to help him escape with all the energy in his soul. And who is the prisoner, once he is found? Surely a healthy, normal, intelligent boy of fourteen did not exist within Paul's mighty walls. Without the walls, he would have had nothing, would have had to rebuild his self from infancy, picking out the pieces of the closet years like shards of glass, carefully, one by one. There was no key I could find that would release him, only the thinnest thread leading inward through his maze, step by agonizing step. And yet, it was so easy to feel that Paul could tell me all the secrets of the universe, that all those years of watching and waiting and burrowing inward had given him knowledge the rest of us could never possess. The belief that there was a way out, a secret door to find . . . it was almost irresistible. And the light never stopped beckoning, giving the lie.

Dan Johnson saw that light and fell into the trap. After the German couple decided they could not adopt Paul, Dan had decided that he would cure Paul himself. He left his wife and family and moved into the guest house with Paul for a month, just the two of them, twenty-four hours a day, alone together in the small space. Dan bathed Paul and fed him and dressed him and talked to him and worked with him and played with him and loved him all day every day for a solid month, searching desperately for the key, for the string, for the way to set free this mystical green-eyed boy, working against time, against puberty, feeling that once Paul passed that barrier alone, he would be lost forever. For thirty days, Dan coaxed and loved and lured, but Paul, damn him, never woke up and said, "Gee, thanks, Dan. You have saved me and I am forever in your debt." Paul refused to get better.

He did learn some things, of course. His receptive language skills improved, Dan said. He could cut his meat with a knife and eat his food properly, with spoon or fork as the meal required, and he could even, every so often, be persuaded to look into another person's face. But the rage and the intelligence remained locked behind the smoky green glass of his eyes.

For this, Paul could not be forgiven. Dan moved back into his own house when the month was up, back to his wife and three children of his own who needed their daddy. And Paul moved back to the RTC. Children like Tracy and Franklin and Katie thrived on the structure, discipline and caring that they received at the RTC. But Paul needed far more attention, more one-to-one intensive twenty-four-hour therapy than the harried RTC staff, dedicated as they were, could provide. Dan Johnson, however, had too much invested in Paul to let him slip away. He could neither bear to see Paul adopted nor see him placed in a more appropriate institution, one that specialized in caring for autistic children. For whatever reason, Dan needed to keep Paul for himself. At the same time, Dan never came to visit; their mutual failure hurt too much. And Paul slipped deeper into himself, and into puberty, until by the time I got there everyone had given up on finding the key, and spent their time instead trying to "socialize" Paul, teaching him not to get angry, not to screech, not to bounce up and down but to sit quietly in a corner. To sit.

I hated what they were doing to Paul. I would watch him, fourteen years old, rocking in the corner with a battered doll, his face hidden against the soft cloth of the doll's body, or bouncing before the mirror on a ball meant for someone half his age and think, my God, what a thing to do to a teenage boy. I wanted him to run, to fill his lungs with air as he shouted, to learn how it felt to be out of breath, to suck up air as a life force, laughing, to scream out his rage at the mountains, to plunge his body into icy water, to roll in the sand on a warm sunny day. He wanted to bounce? Fine, good—then buy him a trampoline, let him bounce higher than anyone ever had. He wanted to scream? Let him scream till it echoed off the canyon, till they heard it in Las Cordilleras, where his parents still lived in their comfortable, two-story house. Paul had so little; at least, I felt, he should be allowed his feelings, rage without bounds, movement at last without restriction, a little bit of the dignity that had been denied him throughout his entire life. He fought for it so desperately, sometimes, screeching with all his might. And always it was "No, Paul! Do you want a timeout?"

But I was just a very junior staff member. A twenty-year-old with no previous experience. I asked once, timidly, whether stifling Paul's anger was really the best way of handling him and was told by Richard, his primary, that of course it was, how else could we socialize him so that he could live in a good institution? Besides, often there was no other way it could have been. Even with one staff member to every three children, the other kids were so demanding that many times there was simply no one available to look after Paul and Corinne. They were so quiet when left alone, so good. They never fought, or caused any trouble. So when Franklin and Tracy and Philip acted up, or ran away, or rumbled with the farm kids, it was always "Just sit there, Paul. Here's a book. Just stay there. Good boy."

I would take Paul with me then, take him on long walks across the fields or around the town, or rock with him, singing, through long, rainy spring afternoons in the playroom. When we were together, I let Paul bounce all he wanted, less concerned about the double standard it would establish for him than about his need to let loose some of his rage. When he pressed his hands to his face, squeezed his eyes shut and screeched, I said "Good, Paul! You're mad! That's it, get good and mad!" In the heat of the summer sun, I made him climb rocks and crawl around the arroyos with me. When he took my hand, a specialized crane, and moved it to a box of cereal he wanted, I told him no, to ask for it or get it himself, and stood my ground, despite all his screeching. And slowly, slowly a bond grew between us. When Paul was upset, the reindeer song could calm him. When he was angry, he knew that if he came to me, I would find a way to help him express it. He would stop his rocking, sometimes, when I sang, to reach up and touch my face. And I would hold him close when he let me, and whisper, I love you, Paul. I love you so so much.

One day I persuaded Lois and Jason to let me take him skiing with the other kids. In the biting wind of the icy mountain, I buckled him into the heavy ski boots and let him clump around in the snow, finally conscious of his feet. He screeched and scrunched up his eyes at me, furious, and I encouraged him to get mad. Other mothers, seeing us, hearing Paul's screams, looked at him pityingly, hey, lady, why are you torturing that child, and I smiled at them sweetly as they shepherded their children to another slope. Paul soon got used to the boots, though, and stopped his screaming, and then Bernie lifted him up and we strapped him onto his skis and pulled him slowly across the ground.

He was silent then, silent and alive, his eyes focused on Bernie's face, legs bent slightly at the knee as he glided across the frozen ground.

But there were many times when I, too, told him to sit quietly with some toy or book, when the other kids were fighting or someone had just run away or when I was simply too tired to cope. Then, far too often, Paul sat, and rocked, and watched the world go by with elfin eyes.

I never lost the feeling that Paul knew what he watched, and why. I always felt that his rage had direction, and that, underneath it lay intelligence and understanding. Through all our walks together, all our songs, I felt the bond between us grow. I felt it when I rocked him, his normally rigid body relaxed against mine. I felt it when I sang to him, and when he touched my face. But I was working against time, too. I had been at Santa Clara almost a year; soon I would have to go back to the real world, my world, a world of ideas, where little boys with cloudy green volcano eyes existed only in textbooks. Paul was going to be abandoned yet again, and the guilt I felt at my impending betrayal of his trust made me pull away sooner than I needed to. Paul sensed my withdrawal, perhaps knew what was coming, he had seen it all before, and he pulled himself away as well, withdrawing, using me, once again, only as a tool.

And then it was the end of December. I had been at the center a year. It was Christmas morning, and we were eating brunch, all the farm kids and RTC kids together for once in peace eating scrambled eggs and blueberry muffins for a Christmas treat in the stained-oak coziness of the Birch Tree Inn. I remember the colors: the golden warmth of the cheesy eggs running into the sky-blue of the blueberry juice, the amber pools of syrup on the pancakes, the mouths of the kids smeared red with raspberry jam as the snow swirled white outside the window, transforming the sagebrush into huge puffs of cotton candy. The kids asked us, "Should we say our prayers?" and bowed their heads sheepishly, Catholic, Protestant, Indian, atheist, murmuring prayers together, crossing themselves, some, and laughing, then lifting their heads again, eating quickly, noisily, happily stealing an occasional sip from the strange slipperiness of an adult's Bloody Mary.

Paul and Corinne sat at a table with me and Jason, stuffing themselves, cramming sausage links and forkfuls of egg into their mouths without tasting them. Across the room, their siblings from the farm sat together at another table with two unfamiliar adults. Peter was talking loudly, his questions carrying across the crowded, noisy room, and the little ones chattered nervously while the older two were silent.

I thought it strange that I had never seen those adults with them before. Over the months I had spent enough time at the farm that I knew most of the staff who worked there if not by name at least by face. But these two did not look like staffers. They must have been in their early forties. The man was pudgy and balding, dressed in a red and black plaid blazer and dark green corduroy pants and cowboy boots. His eyebrows were bushy and strikingly long, growing together across his forehead like a huge worry line. The woman looked like a typical Southwestern housewife. Her hair was a little too blond, almost silvery, coiffed way up on her head. She wore a red party dress with a large gold butterfly brooch pinned above the breast. They seemed strangely oblivious to Peter's questions, and concentrated on the two youngest children, the "normal" ones, who were competing with each other for the adults' attention.

"Who are those people eating with the Hansen kids?" I asked Jason.

He glanced over, then looked back at Paul and Corinne. "Those are their parents," he said. His face was white.

I looked back at the children. The family resemblance was strong. They were all unusually beautiful children, all of them with the fair, creamy skin and dark hair and long lashes. There was Sarah, the oldest, sweet and shy; Eddie, silent, angry, easily capable of breaking the arms and noses of kids who crossed his path; Peter, his desperate questions blocking out the years of guilt he had built up serving as jailer to his younger brother and sister; Tommy and Jill, bright and cute, and, so everyone said, quite normal. Then I looked at the two sitting with me: Corinne, my little porpoise, who sat full at last, her round tummy sticking out over her pants, her head leaning on Joan's shoulder, her hands in her lap, playing with her spit; and Paul, rocking violently in his chair as he stuffed sausage after sausage into his mouth, pausing only to murmur ouiouiouiouioui or snap his hand shut or rock rhythmically in his chair. His green eyes were glazed, forever caged in, no key, no string. And then I looked at his parents, father and mother, bald and bland, suburban and self-satisfied, eating a Christmas brunch with their family.

I wanted to take my knife and plunge it into their eyes, to lock them in a closet for seven years. I felt my throat begin to tighten as the tears sprang into my eyes. "Why don't we go wish them a merry Christmas," I said.

Departure

It has been raining all night and it is raining still, the fat, pregnant drops of a drenching spring rain. I listen to them as they splash off the dirty window of the lecture hall, beating time to the drone of the professor's voice. There is an empty chair to my left, where I have put my jacket and knapsack. The girl on my right wears a long Harris tweed wool coat and has not untied her silvery scarf from around her neck, although it is hot in the room. She writes rapidly in her notebook, the ends of the scarf resting on the edges of the paper, and I wonder why I can find nothing noteworthy. I wonder which of us has missed the point.

I reach over for my knapsack and take out the letter I have received that morning, on my way to this class, and have read only hastily on my walk across the Yard, one eye on the paper and one eye on the mud. It was a bad day to wear my cowboy boots, I think, as I cross my legs and notice that the tips are stained brown from the seeping water. The letter is from my friend Becca, who graduated during the year I was away and took a job working for an Indian rights law firm in the Southwest. My eyes scan the lines until they find the words "are filing suit against a Dan Johnson, who is head of something called the Santa Clara Child Care Center. Have you heard of it?" I read on, and she writes of some kids named Alex and Mike and Paul and Peter, whom she describes from the court record as a "spacey kid who asks a lot of questions." They're the named plaintiffs, she writes, and suddenly I want to cry, because they aren't plaintiffs at all, just sick kids, kids I love. The thing is, she writes, that the Indians wanted their kids back, and this Johnson guy wouldn't let them go. He's prevented other adoptions of Indian kids before, apparently, and so we're suing under the least restrictive environment provisions of the law, and a couple of other violations we found—nothing serious, but it looks like we just might win.

I begin to cough, and the girl next to me looks up in disgust, pulling her scarf closer to her body. I squeeze my eyes shut and listen to the rain, imagine the sky filled with clouds in every color of grey and black, the lightning cutting across the sky like the flash of a sharp knife.

It was clear the night I left the Southwest, still and cold. The air was filled with stars that do not stop at the sky, as they do in the East, but fall all around, as if the sky were a dome, a citadel, strong and protective. I left the children on

New Year's Day, my head pounding from a hangover. I spent the morning riding my horse, a last ride, up and down the arroyos and hills with the town below me quilted in the soft colors of snow and dawn. The air smelled sharp, burning my lungs as we cantered along, and the rising sun cast a shadow of us both on the earth, one black form, the horse and his rider, rocking gently and swiftly down the road. We stopped in a marsh at the bottom of a hill, and listened, silent, to birds playing in the water, startling a family of rabbits when we started on our way again. Harvard, school, this room where I sit now, listening to the rain, felt a million miles away. It still does, even as I hear the professor's voice, as long as I keep my eyes shut and think about the sky.

I look up as the girl next to me stands and excuses herself, brushing against my leg on her way to the aisle. The lecture is over and it is lunchtime, but I do not feel hungry. I feel suddenly unwilling to get wet and decide to stay in here, in the warm, almost cozy room, until the rain stops. I often see a teacher's assistant setting up a projector at the end of my hour and reason that some kind of art class must be next. I like art: the bright colors of the slides looming larger than life on the white screen, when it is too dark to take notes and everyone is forced to think. With difficulty, I make my way against traffic to the back of the lecture hall and curl up like a cat in the leftmost seat in the last row. I see that I am right. The professor comes in and reads a few announcements, and then the room goes dark. I shut my eyes and listen to the hum of the projector, and then

I am back in the mountains again, on that last day, saying good-bye.

I remember going down the mountain to the RTC in my rented red car, driving slowly, my thoughts divided between the sorrow of leaving and the fear of returning. I saw myself, huge, straddling the continent, with one foot stretching toward home and the other still sunk in the Southwestern mud. All my actions that day, all the good-byes, seemed unnaturally slow, as though I were trying to ease that other foot out of the earth, afraid that if I failed, amputation might be necessary, if only to keep some soil between my toes.

It was a lazy day for the kids, a holiday, and so although it was nearly noon when I arrived I found Philip still in his ragged blue bathrobe spooning the last of his breakfast into his mouth and reading the comics aloud to Franklin, who peered over his shoulder and insisted that he knew all the words. Okay, you read to me then, Philip was saying as I walked in, and Franklin said no, he didn't want to, and Philip laughed and there would have been a fight but there I was, and they knew it was the last time they would see me. As it was, I had not seen them since the Christmas brunch, my last official day of work. I had used the week to pack my things and ride my horse and say good-bye to everything I loved there that was not them: the mountains, the friends, the sky. And now I was there to say good-bye to them, too.

They greeted me with a "Hi, Lizard," and competed with each other to tell me the news. I had heard most of it already, floating in the air, but I let them tell me their version anyway. Tracy had left a few days after Christmas: against the better judgment of the staff, and only because she had been at the RTC way past her allotted eighteen months, she had been transferred to a less restrictive center in Los Cordilleras where, according to Lois, she seemed to be doing just fine so far. In her place had come a new little girl, soft and slender, Bernie had told me, with long brown hair, who was now in town with Lois, shopping for some new clothes. There was also a new boy, tall and mean, the kids said, who was now in his room being restrained by Jason because he had blown up and thrown Franklin across the livingroom during the morning meeting. "I'm okay, though," Franklin said, "and I didn't even lose my temper." I smiled at him and gave him a hug.

Franklin said, "Come with me," and took me down the hall, past the new boy's faceless screams, to his room, where he carefully removed a piece of paper from a blue three-ring binder and handed it to me. I saw that it was covered with words, and at the top of the page there was a gold star and the words "100%! Excellent!" written in red ink. Franklin kept a finger on it as I held it, unwilling to let go of his achievement. I looked down at him, the black hair and brown cheeks pushed up in a smile, and felt that I wanted to hold him forever. I knew that I would never see him again, and I wondered if that made him sad. He told me that he thought he was going to make it, even back with his family. I hope he is right.

We went back into the kitchen, and Philip brought in the clock he got for Christmas. It was digital, its numbers made of liquid crystal, shining red in its black face. It told the time down to the tenth of a second, just like his watch. He ran it through its different functions, showing me the different alarms, the calendar, the special calculator function. His eyes were bright with excitement, the magic of control, of mastery, and I wondered if he would ever dare to live with such imprecise machines as people are. Again, I felt a stab of regret and longing that I would not be around to find out. I felt as though I had been reading a fascinating and wonderful book, in which the characters are drawn so well they seem almost real, so real that I have grown to love them, and that now the book was being torn out of my hands before I could read the ending. I told him it looked great, and he smiled and said yeah, and then began to ask about Harvard, and was I glad to be going back.

The slide changes and I shift in my seat, trying to get comfortable. I look at the straight brown hair of the person sitting in front of me and have a sudden urge to reach out and stroke it. The sound of the rain is lighter and less regular, and I think that it must be letting up, although I can't really see a window from where I am sitting. I decide I will leave at the end of this class.

I sat in the kitchen that day, wondering how I would answer Philip's question. Was I glad to be going back? I felt that it was time. I missed the ocean, and the way the glass-flecked pavement caught the light as I walked down the hot summer city streets. I missed my father, and the way he came home all sweaty after tennis and lay in his icy air-contioned room and ate a grapefruit, dribbling the juice on his chest. I missed my mother, riding on her bicycle to the grocery store and coming back laden with food for me to eat. And I missed my friends, and the simple, selfish life of staying up late talking about Shakespeare and Plato and all the things that were so irrelevant in the sunshine on the mountains. Yet I knew that once I was back with those things I would miss the life I had here: the children's hugs, the honesty of emotion, the safety of this house in which you could lose control and know that someone would be there to stop you before you went too far.

But before I could begin to answer him, Jason walked in and greeted me and said, "Whew, you're getting out just in time, this new guy looks like a toughie, so how're you doing, Frank-o?" And we ate together in the warmth of the kitchen, ate special deluxe burgers with cheese in the middle that Jason fried up for us in the oversized, cast-iron frying pan, and then it was time to say good-bye. I went to them, one after the other, hugging first Philip then Jason then Franklin, squeezing them hard, to imprint the feel of their bodies on my arms. I went to hug Corinne, too, but she was eating, and moaned when I came near. And then I went to Paul. He sat at the table, flapping his hand in front of his face, noisily chewing on his hamburger. I bent down to see into his eyes, but he looked away. I hugged him anyway, and said softly, "I love you, Paul," but his expression did not change. It was like hugging the wood of a rocking chair.

Then Bernie came in and said, "Come talk to me a minute," and we went inside and I felt the strength of his arms pressing me into his body, the gentle scratch of his beard against my face. "I love you," he said, and I ached inside with the pressure of holding back the words, "I love you, too," because they were not true. So I said, "Take care of yourself," instead, and let him squeeze me tighter, as I had felt myself clutch the others a few minutes before. "I'll miss you," I said, and felt myself beginning to cry. He straightened, then, and pushed me away. "Hasta la bye-bye," he said.

I walked out of the kitchen and into the yard, rubbing my hands over Abraham's back and letting him lick my face. "Good dog," I said. Then I got in my car and drove off, retracing my steps to the airport in Las Cordilleras. I waved to them until I could no longer see them, and in the rearview mirror I saw Franklin and Philip wave back, Philip's hand grazing Franklin's face with each arc of his arm.

The slide changes again, and I try to think of the things I gained. I learned many things, in my year in the mountains: to light a wood stove, to eat jalapeños, to roast a chili, to accept other people's anger without letting it rule my life, to ride a horse, to love a child who cannot love back. I remember coming home in the airplane, crowded with tired-looking grown-ups and cranky children, more people in that small plane than had been in my entire town. I wondered whether I was going home or leaving it, and finally decided that both could be home, each a part of me, making me whole. I had felt so strong then, aware of my body filling up space, feeling the smoothness of the pen in my fingers and the rough of the sweater against my neck. I remember getting off the plane, too, and the tight, fierce hugs of my parents, the joyful ones of my friends. The world seemed simple. If Harvard were a puzzle, then I had found the missing pieces in the mountains, and it would at last all fit together as it should have all along.

I look around me, at the heads bent over notebooks in the semigloom, and think, No, it has not been that simple. It is all well and good in the abstract to learn to accept anger, but a friend's angry stare bores holes through my defenses still, and wounds. It is all well and good to have two homes, but I find that no one seems interested in straddling them with me. I am often lonely, and wonder whether it is a price I will always have to pay. I shift in my seat again, and sigh. The man next to me asks me to please be quiet. I think I am not louder than the noise of the rain, and then notice that the rain has stopped. I do not know what I gained. I do not even know what the children gained. Yet I am not sorry I went. I smile and feel myself smiling in the dark.

The lights go on in the room again, and the professor begins to talk about light and color and composition and form. Tired of thinking, I listen. "See, people," he says, "look at the way her robe is draped around her legs, how it falls to the floor, filling the foreground of the canvas and setting her back, apart." He talks about the symbols the class has seen in the picture, the basin and towel illustrating the purity of the Virgin, the candle on the table extinguished by the greater light of God, the split window in the background, open to heaven, closed to earth. "It is a remarkable painting," the professor says, "but primitive. The artist had never studied in Italy, he did not know of the new conventions. I will show you," the professor says, and he asks for the lights to be dimmed once more. On the new slide he shows us, straight lines have been superimposed over the painting, starting from the edges of the canvas and running along the artist's diagonals, the forms getting smaller to show depth as the painter takes us back into the room. "Ever since the Renaissance," the professor says, "artists have known how to make the perspective right, so that all the lines meet and disappear at the same point. But look here," he says, "in this painting the lines cross each other; there are at least a dozen separate depth diagonals." He nods his head and switches the light on abruptly. "You see," he says, "there is no vanishing point perspective."

The lecture is over, and I gather up my knapsack and coat. The man next to me squeezes by, glaring. I wait until the room has emptied of all except three students, who stand near the professor's podium, talking to him with flushed faces as he collects his notes. Then slowly I walk through the room and out into the soft, damp warmth of the Yard. The sky is clearing, and the beads of water on the new leaves catch the light. I turn left and head home, toward my dorm, trying, in my cowboy boots, to avoid the mud.

Epilogue

In the end, my friend's firm won their suit against Dan Johnson and Santa Clara. By order of the state, the farm was closed, although the RTC was allowed to stay open.

I do not know whether that verdict was right or wrong. Surely Dan Johnson did many things I did not agree with, but just as surely he provided a loving home for most of the hundred children who had not had one before, and may not now. On starry nights I think of them, and wonder how they are. I think of Alex, betrayed yet again, by all of us who told him to the best of our too-limited foresight that he had finally come home. I do not know where he is now, but I am sure he will not be able to trust again. I wonder whether Philip, wherever he is, is allowed to use his liquid crystal clock or whether even time has lost its magic. I think of Franklin, writhing in Richard's arms, now probably back home with the brothers who will beat him still, a tamed lion sent back to the wild. I think of Jesse and Joe, back on the streets, and Tony in an institution for the mentally retarded. I wonder where Mike is, and why Dan did not adopt him, too. I think of Tracy, who did not last long in the center in Las Cordilleras, I heard, and was sent to the state lock-up ward, and of James, flowering, perhaps, in the perpetual warmth of southern California, with his sister who finally agreed to take him, after all. I think of sullen Lee, too, eating Vienna sausages in the trailer, and Katie safe and sound with her family. I think of Bernie, who wrote to tell me that he had run over Abraham in his truck as he came home from work, killing him, and I wonder whether it is true or whether he said it merely to hurt me, to get back at me for leaving him. And I think of the Hansens, picture Peter howling his questions to the wind, never finding the answer he needs, Corinne floating her life away in the warm bath that will never be the womb she so desperately seeks, and Paul, the heartbeat, seeing and knowing us all, silently and endlessly rocking, somewhere.

I cried the day I read the verdict and took out all my old pictures and diaries. And in the back of one, stuffed away between pages, I found their poem.

JAPANESE POETRY LAND

There once was a martian
That didn't exist.
People in there running
With its radiant beauty
And all the pretty colors.
An ex-swastika.
God is coming to earth

And the sun is mad.
Blue oogalog bug comes running
And Chinamen are scared.
Spaceships are running
With beautiful skies
Racing through the marsh.
All the trees are running for safety
Just as dawn was breaking
And the martians are a snob.
Milk and ice cream
Martians
And the mountains are sneaking
Just as the sun was peaking.
Everything goes back to normal again.
There are green trees in the forest.
Martian got back into the airplane.
The martian's looking at you.
The world started over.